"Video games are fun and exciting. For some, however, the games take over their lives. Olivia and Kurt Bruner's important book is the first to shine light on the secret scourge of video game addiction."

—David Walsh, PhD, president, National Institute on Media and the Family and author of *Why Do They Act That Way*

"An exceptionally helpful book for parents. Convincing, confessing, and constructive. Points parents, teachers, and youth workers to a very real danger facing our children today."

—Dr. Archibald D. Hart, senior professor of psychology, Fuller Theological Seminary

"Addiction is a terrible life waster. Busy parents are caught up short when addiction to seemingly innocent play—like a computer game—turns out to be a serious spoiler. One out of five kids becomes addicted to either computer or video games, captured in an unreal world where human relationships and normal responsibilities become irrelevant. In college dormitories across the country an astounding number of students become dropouts, skipping classes, missing exams and deadlines while the game pulls them onward. The hours fly by! Because the games take skill, parents may boast about how clever their young children are at games. It's a harmless way to keep children absorbed and 'out of your hair.' PLAYSTATION NATION warns the reader that more may be happening than you now see. Olivia and Kurt Bruner know what they are talking about—both from experience and professional data. Listen up!"

—Gladys Hunt, author of *Honey for a Child's Heart* and *Honey for a Teen's Heart*

"I can't think of a single parent I've met who would hand their child a snake if they knew it was poisonous. (Or in most cases, a snake of any kind!) But what if that same device that 'keeps our kids busy' while we do all our important things, actually came with a 'bite'? You simply must read this book before or if you're in the video game stage of your child's life. It's not all bad news—but it's wise words on making sure a toy doesn't become a trap for a much-loved son or daughter."

—John Trent, Ph.D., president and founder of The Center for StrongFamilies and author of *The Two Degree Difference* and *Breaking the Cycle of Divorce*

302 F m
2.231
Bru

Authors' Note: All names except the authors' family's names have been changed to protect the privacy of the contributors.

Copyright © 2006 by Olivia and Kurt Bruner

All rights reserved.

Center Street

Hachette Book Group USA

1271 Avenue of the Americas, New York, NY 10020

Visit our Web site at www.centerstreet.com.

Center Street is a division of Hachette Book Group USA. The Center Street name and logo are trademarks of Hachette Book Group USA.

Printed in the United States of America

First Edition: September 2006

10 9 8 7 6 5 4 3 2 1

Library of Congress Cataloging-in-Publication Data

Bruner, Olivia.

Playstation nation : protect your child from video game addiction / Olivia Bruner and Kurt Bruner.—1st ed.

p. cm.

Includes bibliographical references.

ISBN-13: 978-1-931722-74-2

ISBN-10: 1-931722-74-9

1. Video games and children. 2. Video gamers—Psychology. I. Bruner, Kurt D. II. Title.

HQ784.V53B78 2006

302.23'1—dc22   2006008179

PLAYSTATION NATION

PROTECT YOUR CHILD FROM VIDEO GAME ADDICTION

OLIVIA BRUNER AND KURT BRUNER

CENTER
STREET®

CENTER STREET
NEW YORK   BOSTON   NASHVILLE

ACKNOWLEDGMENTS

The journey behind this book owes a debt to several wonderful folks I wish to thank for their encouragement and support, including . . .

- Vicki and Thomas Griffin. This book is as much your story as ours.
- Those interviewed for the true confession chapters. Your vulnerability will no doubt help many avoid similar mistakes.
- Tori, who heard most of this manuscript walking next to me on the treadmill and forwarded many helpful e-mails and news clips along the way; Sarah, who cheered me on when I wanted to back off from such a controversial subject; and other dear friends who provided an idea, a question, or a nudge at just the right moment.

- Chip MacGregor. You believed in this project first.
- Chris Park. You pushed us to produce a better manu-script—for which our readers will certainly be glad!
- And our children, who have patiently endured our time away from them, and their own time away from video games.

Olivia Bruner

TO KYLE

Your maturity made this book possible.

CONTENTS

FOREWORD

S IMPLY PUT, CONSIDER the warnings and advice in
this book the equivalent of an insurance policy for
your heart-felt desire to have a highly healthy child.

If you have a child who plays video games (or may in the
future play video games), shut the cover of this book now,
march up to the check-out counter at this moment, and purchase it. Immediately. Period.

But if you're not convinced by my recommendation, then at
least consider this: imagine it's a dark, stormy night. The kids
are in bed and you are about to turn in for the evening. The
rain is coming down in sheets and lightning is crackling all
around. The thunder shakes the windows. It's creepy and scary.

Then you are startled by a loud knock on your front door.

You put on a robe and scurry to the door. After turning on
the front porch light, you look out through the window and

see a scruffy stranger who appears to have neither shaved nor bathed in several days. He has an unlit cigar stuck in his mouth and is wearing a hat with water dripping off the rim. His oilskin raincoat is soaked and dirty and his shoes look like they had better days many years ago.

"Can I help you?" you call through the door—not daring to open it.

"Yeah!" he calls back. "I'm here to educate and entertain your children. Mind if I come in, go to their bedroom, and spend some time with 'em?"

I need a quick decision from you. Option one: Open the door and say, "By all means, head on back to their room. And be sure to close the bedroom door behind you. Don't worry, I won't be in to check on you all." Option two: Call 911 and get the police there ASAP.

What an incredibly silly question, right? No parent in his or her right mind would choose option one, correct?

Well, believe it or not, most parents in America *are* choosing option one by allowing electronic intruders—dangerous strangers—unfriendly aliens—vicious visitors—into their children's bedrooms in the form of video games.

Consider several realities.

A large 2005 study by the Kaiser Family Foundation found that the total amount of media content young people are exposed to each day has increased by more than an hour over the past five years—now topping eight and a half hours per day—with most of the increase coming from video games.[1] That's the equivalent of a full-time job!

The growth in video games has been explosive over the last decade. Over 80 percent of children have at least one video game console at home—and over half of these are in the child's bedrooms, where it is all but impossible for parents to monitor them.[2]

The Culture and Family Institute reports, "The deadliest school shooting in history occurred in Hartford, Germany, on April 26, 2002. There a student, mimicking the shooter from the [video] game *Counter Strike,* went to school dressed in special ops clothing, opened fire, and killed thirteen teachers, two students, and himself. Police later found fifty-two sniper-style video games at his home."

The Bruners will show you there are many, many other ways a child who spends time every day in front of a video game or computer screen can be negatively impacted by the activity. In fact, I would argue that your child and family have a nearly 100 percent chance of being influenced and impressed *negatively* by video games.

Olivia and Kurt have dedicated themselves to demonstrating to you why our children have become obsessed with video games, and what you should know to help your child avoid addiction to what they call "the digital drug."

This is a heart-rending book born out of their pain and personal experiences as they attempted to wrestle with the addictive nature of video games in the lives of their own kids. Their experiences and research have given them the heart-felt desire to help you and your spouse face the difficult questions raised by aggressive marketing and advertising of the digital game industry—not to mention the incredible peer pressure to which your child will likely be subjected—especially your boy(s).

We know that the more video time a child has, the worse their health is in almost every measure. Increased video time increases your child's risk of obesity and all the diseases that come with it. Dr. William Dietz of the Centers for Disease Control says, "Almost anything uses more energy than watching TV."[3] Ditto for video games. And the more time your child spends in front of a video screen, the less time he or she will spend interacting with brothers or sisters—and with you.[4]

I could go on and on, but I bet you are getting the point.

If your child is being lured away from normal, healthy childhood activities into a digital universe, this book is for you.

The video game epidemic is a serious one—with longterm consequences, not only for our society, but also for your child and your family.

Every parent wants his or her kids to become happy, healthy, productive adults. The Bruners argue forcefully that that goal is far more difficult to achieve in a Playstation Nation.

When it comes to setting down and enforcing video-time rules—or considering the decision to become a video-game–free home, this book will show you how not to be a shrinking violet. It will show you how to be disciplined as you lovingly train your child. It will argue that "It is easier to indulge a child than to shape his character."

Yet there are signs of hope. You've picked up this book.

After you purchase and read it, you'll be equipped to join the parents who, for a variety of healthy reasons, have created an intentional strategy for dealing with video games in the home—or, eliminating them from the home. And, as you do so, you'll be joining a rapidly growing group of parents making wise video decisions for the children they have the obligation and responsibility to nurture and raise up into highly healthy young adults.

Some do it to promote family closeness, to better control what their children are exposed to, to stimulate their children's dreams and creativity, or to protect and nurture their children.

Still others have found that video-game- and TV-free children actually show a very high degree of relational health. They are more likely to participate in sit-down dinners, family activities, hobbies, board and sports games, chores, pet care, walking, music, gardening, going to movies, sleeping, sports, community service, housecleaning, outdoor activities, and writing.[5]

I have no question that children whose parents allow their "umbilical cords" to remain connected to video games and unlimited Internet access will suffer serious consequences. Children who are freed from the lure of video games, on the other hand, will be shown to have a longer attention span and improved grades at school. I believe children who are freed from the compulsion for (or even addiction to) video games will be more active physically and more healthy than other children their age.

Get ready for a highly enlightening and sometimes scary read. Be prepared to be shocked. Plan to learn. Make ready for tidal changes in your family. To have highly healthy kids in the arena of their video game habits, you can do no less.

Walt Larimore, M.D.
Colorado Springs, CO
February 2006
www.DrWalt.com

INTRODUCTION

EMILY AWOKE UPON hearing a noise downstairs. It was two o'clock in the morning. Only minutes earlier she had been sleeping, exhausted from another busy day managing a household dominated by the activities and antics of adolescent boys—including the never-ending battle over video games. Her sons protested that she was too strict when she limited playtime to one hour per day. She saw them as obsessed when they pushed for every possible minute in front of that darn box. Emily hated the zombielike persona that overtook her boys during play, and wanted them to spend their time doing more productive, healthy activities.

Now, nervously pulling back the blanket, she got out of bed and slipped quietly from her room toward the mysterious sound. Anxiety bled into anger as she approached the faint but distinct music of the boys' favorite video game—the same game they had been ordered to stop playing hours earlier in order to go to bed. They had once again passed their allotted time. Despite their mom's persistent urging to "shut off that game," they pleaded for permission to finish one more level. After reluctantly hitting the pause button, the boys had decided to sneak out of bed later to finish what they had started.

Caught in the act, the boys tried to explain that they were only playing "tomorrow's time allowance." It didn't help.

At that moment Emily couldn't decide whether to scream or cry; whether she was losing her mind or coming to her senses. She told the boys to stay put and walked back up the stairs. She paced back and forth in her room for fifteen or twenty minutes, cooled down, and gathered her wits as she wondered how to respond. Emily had already spent months trying to limit video game playtime—withholding the game when chores or homework went undone, and trying to convince her sons that there were better ways to spend their time. None of her efforts had worked—her boys' obsession had grown stronger by the day. And at this moment it struck her: "If I don't get rid of that game system tonight, I might never do it."

With deliberate intent Emily unplugged her boys' video game system, gathered up cords and sundry devices, walked onto her second-story deck, and pitched hundreds of dollars' worth of equipment over the railing. With a great sense of relief she listened for the sweet sound of crashing electronics below. "There!" she assured herself. "That should take care of the problem."

Her four boys watched in horror, pleading with her to stop—in sheer disbelief that she would go so far off the deep end as to destroy their prized possession and hoping one last time she would give in to their pleading. But Mom had passed the point of negotiating deals. This time they had gone too far!

Years later Emily told me and my husband that this decision was the turning point, with lasting implications for her sons' lives. Her oldest, for example, went to college with seven friends, all of whom had developed a similar obsession with video games as kids. None of their moms, however, had experienced Emily's dramatic awakening to the problem. The result? Too much game time and too little studying in the dorms led to four of the seven eventually dropping out of school to get part-time jobs—freeing up more time for video games. But Emily's son was not one of them. Her 2 a.m. decision saved her boys from an obsession that is stealing countless children and adults away from real life.

Emily's emotional ordeal reflects those shared by a growing number of parents concerned that video games have become their child's singular life obsession. Few go to the extreme of tossing their system over a second-story deck, but many have felt a similar urge.

Shannon, for example, was troubled by how much time her seventh-grade son, Jeremy, played video games. After years of owning various systems and journeying into the bottomless pit of potential titles and levels, Jeremy had lost interest in nearly all other activities, despite living on a large property with endless opportunities for boyhood adventures. Shannon used a very different strategy with her son: she offered to buy him an engine-powered go-kart if he got rid of his games. The decision was an extremely difficult one for Jeremy, who cried as he said farewell to his virtual entertainment box. Now he enjoys driving his go-kart as well as many other activities. And Mom considers that motorized toy one of the best investments she's ever made: "Getting rid of video games released Jeremy to explore other interests— and he found many that he now loves, including drama, music, and outdoor activities."

No matter how they decide to handle it, more and more parents are finding it necessary to intervene as they observe the influence of video games on their children and teens. What's going on? How did a seemingly harmless entertainment option become such an overbearing part of our children's lives? Why did a local home builder, hailing a development that had enough outdoor activities to keep kids active, invite potential buyers to "discover a place where video games are never played"? Could it be that parents dream of such a place after having tried everything else to move their children into real-life pursuits?

This book is dedicated to discovering why our children

have become obsessed with video games and what parents should know to help their children avoid addiction to what I call the digital drug.

Playstation Nation

It all began with a tiny dot blipping back and forth on a black screen between two white dashes simulating table tennis paddles. *Pong,* amazingly boring by today's digital game standards, mesmerized families during the late 1970s and early 1980s. At around the same time, my personal favorite, *Pac-Man,* allowed me to chase and devour little mushroom-shaped guys around an electronic maze. Those were the good old days when video games seemed nothing more than innocent fun.

Today things are very different. A growing body of parents and educators, myself included, are concerned about a drug-like problem that has emerged over the past two decades: the obsession our kids have with video games. This book grows out of personal experience in trying to deal with the addictive nature of video games in the lives of my own kids and a desire to help moms and dads face difficult questions raised by the aggressive emergence of the digital game industry:

- Should I buy my child a game system?
- How much should I restrict my child's playtime?
- How do I handle the unending push for more time and better games?

- Why don't my children want to do or talk about anything else?
- Is it risky to let my adolescent spend time playing online games?
- How do I get my kids to turn off their virtual game box and enjoy real life?

For us the process began when our oldest son prominently listed a computerized game system at the top of his Santa list. We resisted for some time, concerned Kyle might become obsessed like other kids we'd seen—unable to talk about anything but the latest video games, bored by the notion of playing outdoors, sports, Lego, board games, or other child activities, and generally apathetic toward real-life pursuits. But when friends offered us their old system, we hesitantly accepted—determined we would limit time played so that it remained a small part of an overall balanced lifestyle.

Before long, however, we noticed our once-active son being enticed away from normal, healthy childhood activities into a digital universe. Board games remained on the shelf. Outdoor activities decreased. Even relationships with friends and family were affected, dominated by game chatter or conflict over why he couldn't play for "just one more level." Most parents give up or give in to what seems a pointless battle. For my husband and me, however, the cycle forced a critical point of decision. But first we decided to research the world of games in order to make the most informed possible decision on if and when to allow our children to play.

This book grows out of our desire to help other parents avoid the mistakes we've made. Few people realize that the computer and video game compulsion overtaking children, especially boys, indicates much more than childish fun. It is a serious epidemic with long-term consequences, feeding patterns of addiction that—unlike the next level of a game—are difficult to beat.

Pinball Wizards

In 1969 the Who produced a hit song titled "Pinball Wizard," celebrating a relatively recent adolescent phenomenon—the video arcade. Dark halls filled with digital bells and whistles became the gathering point for unsupervised teens looking to pass time in a manner considered seedy at best—the juvenile equivalent of a pool hall. No good parent, it was understood, dropped off her child at a video arcade to spend hours playing pinball. At best, it was considered a waste of time and money. At worst, an unwholesome influence.

How times have changed. No longer regarded as a waste of time and money, we now consider game systems an essential entertainment investment. Rather than an unwholesome influence, they are commended as a way to keep kids out of trouble. In some ways they do, but at what cost?

> Game systems are commended as a way to keep kids out of trouble. In some ways they do, but at what cost?

In 1969 good mothers steered kids clear of the arcade. Today good mothers buy kids their very own systems.

In 1970 kids became the local pinball wizard through high-score bragging rights. Today kids strive to best their peers by conquering game levels.

In the early days of digital sport, guns were used to shoot innocent fowl in games like *Duck Hunt.* Today they are used to shoot police officers in top-selling games like *Grand Theft Auto.*

When I was a teen, adolescent boys were tempted by the silhouette of seductive women drawn on the background of pinball scoreboards. Now preadolescent boys are presented with the option of digital group sex. A recent advertisement for the best-selling computer game *Sims 2* pictures a wife returning home from business travel. She is surprised to discover her husband in bed with two young women. The player is given five options. Should the wife scream, divorce, punch, cry, or join? Any idea which of the five options hormone-driven preteens might select? The ad invites prospective buyers to "satisfy primal urges" using life-choice scenarios, including the picture of a man with a blonde bombshell on his lap with a mostly undressed brunette observer—bearing the caption "Meet the woman of your dreams. Introduce her to your wife." Moral relevance at its best!

Such games extolling virtual vice are available at nearly every family retail establishment, including Wal-Mart, Target, and Blockbuster Video. Once restricted to the domain of dark halls filled with unsupervised adolescents, sex and violence have gone mainstream.

How mainstream? Believe it or not, the video game industry has surpassed the movie industry, boasting annual revenue of over $23 billion in 2003—and according to Worldwide Market Forecasts for the Video Game and Interactive Entertainment Industry, is projected to top $33 billion by 2008,[1] making it one of the most consistent influences in the lives of this generation of kids. According to a study conducted by the Kaiser Family Foundation in 2005, over 80 percent of young people have at least one video game console at home—half of them in their bedrooms, where it is all but impossible for parents to monitor play. And that does not include the countless households where kids access PC-based computer and Internet games, some of which can be far more insidious than those sold for Nintendo and PlayStation.

Despite this industry's relative infancy, growth has been explosive, sneaking up on unsuspecting parents who once associated video games with the bygone innocence of *Pong* and *Pac-Man*. But the emerging trends indicate anything but playful innocence and harmless fun. Consider the following:

- According to experts like David Walsh, PhD, spokesman for the American Medical Association's media violence campaign, one out of five kids were addicted to computer and video games in 2002.[2]
- The National Institute on Media and the Family, a nonprofit organization for parents, provides warning signs for

computer and video game addiction, outlining a common scenario when "a fantasy world on-line or in a game has replaced his or her real world. The virtual reality of the computer or game is more inviting than the everyday world of family, school or work. With the increased access to pornography on the Internet and in games, this fantasy world may be highly sexual."[3]

One out of five kids are addicted to computer and video games.

- A 2002 report from CBS News uncovers the tragic tale of Shawn Woolley, a once-happy kid who shot himself fatally while sitting in front of his computer. On the screen was the game *EverQuest*. "He shot himself because of the game," said Liz, Shawn's grieving mom. Liz is one of hundreds claiming that *EverQuest* addictions have ruined—or taken—the lives of loved ones.

Such reports highlight the challenge we face as parents, driven home during conversations we've had with friends who dislike the influence video games are having on their children, but who feel that restricting or eliminating access is unreasonable in a culture where every child plays.

So goes the parental pickle. On one hand, the kids complain of ill treatment when we restrict game time. On the other, we fear their possible addiction, not to mention feeling there must be a better way kids could spend their time. What's a parent to do? This book is our way of helping moms and dads take an objective look at the data and stories associated with what has become a major parental concern. We will summarize the consensus of a growing body of research on the physiological and emotional realities that pull some kids toward game addiction. We will share lessons learned while interviewing parents and kids who have experienced the good and bad of electronic games—and have made different choices in response. And we will provide practical advice and ideas gleaned along the way, including suggestions for alternative activities.

Be forewarned. We found no "one size fits all" solution to this topic, no cookie-cutter plan. One thing, however, is clear. The pattern of addiction associated with electronic games is real, and a threat to the well-being of your child. Other families will make choices very different from our own because each child and every family dynamic is unique. But choices must be made, and they will have consequences.

Before diving in, we should note that when we refer to video games, we include computer, handheld, and many Internet-based games because they can share the same basic functionality and play patterns. There are exceptions to the rule, including certain computer-based educational games and some group-oriented party games.

It should also be noted that the video game industry changes so fast that the specific examples in this book will be outdated within weeks of publication. Newer, more sophisticated games come out every year, making it impossible to stay on top of every development. One thing is certain, however. If the trend detailed in these pages continues, games will be more and more addictive, not less. Our Web site and e-newsletter will offer the latest information as it becomes available. Check it out at www.VideoGameTrouble.org.

For ease of reading, Kurt and I have written this book in my voice (Olivia's). I hope you find these pages helpful as you shepherd your child through the complex and confusing questions all parents must face as they deal with the growing tidal wave of video game addiction.

CHAPTER

1

OUR STORY

I N 1996 I knew what to do. If only I had listened to myself.

Kyle came of age in a child's world enamored with the bleeps and bounds of a super little guy named Mario and other popular Nintendo marvels. Only five years old, he could not resist the excitement such games promised. I don't recall where he first encountered his passion for digital games. It could have been any of a dozen places: a friend's home, the Media Play store where he watched older boys play while I shopped for books, or perhaps sitting next to a car-pool buddy who was playing one of the portable gadgets that evolved into the now-omnipresent Game Boy.

Truth be told, I paid little attention at the time to the emerging dominance of video games—consumed by the endless duties of mothering two boys—and was only vaguely aware of the growing influence this industry had in the culture at large, including my first child's activity wish list.

I do remember feeling wary of the trend. In fact, on more than one occasion my neighbor and close friend Sarah and I had discussed whether to allow our kids to own a game system. With only a few months' difference in age between our boys, both of us had an uneasy feeling. We had seen the emerging symptoms in other kids: the entranced stare, the irritability when asked to stop playing, the temper tantrums when made to stop. We didn't like what we saw, and didn't want to see it in our little angels.

"I don't think I'll ever buy Kyle a game system," I recall sharing with Sarah.

"Neither will I," she agreed. "I don't like how kids act while they play them."

But that was about the extent of our conversation. Naive to what the next few years would bring, it was not yet a major issue for either of us.

Wise Counsel?

As he approached six years old, Kyle became increasingly interested in video games. Soon the occasional game at the arcade and watching at the bookstore were no longer enough, and he began asking me to let him play at home. Seduced by that sweet kindergarten voice and irresistible puppy dog eyes, I considered the possibility. But first, I determined, I needed some wise counsel from more experienced moms.

I began with my sister Terri. I had long admired her maternal skills raising my then adolescent nephew Nicholas. Nick seemed like a well-adjusted, intelligent, polite young man with balanced interests. He did not own the latest and greatest video game system, but he did play.

"He likes Nintendo," Terri said, "but it has not become all-consuming like it does with other kids." Good news, it seemed; not every kid turned into a demoniac when allowed to play. What had Terri done to avoid that trap?

"I limit the time he can spend," she explained, "which hasn't been a problem, since Nick likes other activities—reading, games, watching television—you know, the usual."

More good news. Kyle liked reading, games, television, and other "usual" things. I made a note to self: "Keep his interests diverse and all should be well."

I also approached Julie, the mother of Jonathan, another well-adjusted, intelligent, polite young man with balanced interests. I remembered that Jonathan, a homeschooled kid, owned a Super Nintendo game system, so I assumed Julie knew something about how to avoid the pitfalls.

"I don't like Jonathan playing those games," Julie admitted. "But we are strict about how much time he can spend, and we use it as a tool to motivate him. When he completes his schoolwork, he gets an hour of playtime. It seems to work pretty well."

Second note to self: "Game systems can be used to motivate success in school."

I wondered whether Julie had observed any of the unpleasant side effects in Jonathan that she and I had criticized in other kids.

"Jonathan is a good kid. But we have had our conflicts, especially when I tell him it is time to quit. And I don't like the themes or images in some of the games—especially the more violent ones."

Despite her relatively minor concerns, however, it seemed that Jonathan had accepted Julie's restrictions and honored her parameters. Another green light as I considered Kyle's requests.

Innocent Beginnings

I will never forget the excited glee on Kyle's face the first time I decided to rent a Nintendo system from Blockbuster. Kurt and I were leaving town for the weekend. Knowing that the energy of our older friends who were babysitting did not match our boys', we decided to make it easy on them by renting a system to keep the kids occupied part of the time. It was our first baby step in relaxing my formerly puritanical standards.

I took seven-year-old Kyle with me to rent the games. While perusing the various titles, he struck up a conversation with the store clerk, a boy who appeared about eighteen years old.

"My mommy is letting me rent Nintendo for the weekend!" came Kyle's excited proclamation. "She won't let me buy Nintendo. That's why we have to rent it."

A bit embarrassed, I turned to engage in the dialogue, intending to explain the reasons I had decided to deprive my son of something most kids considered an essential part of the happy American childhood. Before I could say anything, however, the young man made an insightful and ultimately prophetic statement.

"Be glad your mommy doesn't let you buy one." It was the last thing I expected to hear from a teenage boy. "I had one when I was young," he continued. "I remember rushing through my schoolwork because I wanted to get to my Nintendo. I did my chores so that I could play some more. It is all I ever thought about."

Moments later Kyle and I walked out of the store with our rented system and games. He was eager to play; I was duly warned.

When Kurt and I returned from our trip, we discovered just how easily "part of the time" could become a child's sole, consuming interest. The boys had spent almost every waking moment staring into the screen, defeating levels and conquering worlds. They couldn't have been happier, excitedly describing highlights of their adventures with the Mario Brothers and Donkey Kong. Like every other part of his life, Kyle wanted Mom and Dad to pay attention to his chatter and celebrate his accomplishments. After all, he had defeated almost every level!

> The boys spent almost every waking moment staring into the screen, defeating levels and conquering worlds.

For some reason, neither of us felt particularly good about the revelation.

Trojan Horse

Over the next several years Kyle enjoyed periodic but brief Nintendo excursions, usually tied to some special occasion: weekend rentals for a birthday celebration; seasonal stints to keep the kids occupied during spring, winter, and summer school breaks; and the occasional vacation with friends who offered him the joys of older games, including *Mario 2, Tetris,* and the ever-popular *Duck Hunt.* Neither Kurt nor I liked the influence the games seemed to have on Kyle. But we could return or leave them whenever we wanted, with no worries.

One day, however, the worries came to stay.

I should point out that the primary reason we gave our kids for renting rather than owning a game system was financial. We "couldn't afford" Nintendo—an excellent cover for our unspoken concern that ownership might turn our precious firstborn into who knew what type of kid.

Imagine our dilemma when friends offered to give us their old system. Of course, they made the offer in front of our wide-eyed boys, eliminating any possibility of graciously declining. And so, just like that, the Trojan horse entered our home.

When you merely rent a game system, you believe you do not need to be overly strict. After all, goes the logic, the whole problem gets boxed up and returned after a few days. So, you think, let them have their fun. But when a Super Nintendo unit sits beside your television screaming out the names of your children twenty-four hours a day, seven days a week, you face a much more challenging dynamic. All of those well-intentioned rationalizations for ownership quickly melt away, replaced by the daily conflicts of childhood pleading and parental threats. I can't tell you how often the following drama occurred over the next few years.

> **KYLE:** Can I play Nintendo?
> **MOM:** Have you finished your schoolwork and practiced your piano?
> **KYLE:** Can't I play first?
> **MOM:** You know the rules.

Motivated by the prospect of digital delights, Kyle hurriedly completes his tasks.

> **KYLE:** I'm done. Can I play now?

Feeling pretty good that my "reward system" rationale is working, I approve, referencing my second restriction.

Mom: Okay. But you need to set the timer for thirty minutes so that you can take a bath before bed.

Distracted by other duties and pleased that Kyle is occupied, I lose track of time. Suddenly, I notice that an hour has passed.

Mom: Kyle, are you still playing Nintendo?
Kyle: Yes, Mom.
Mom: It has been an hour. I told you to set the timer for thirty minutes!
Kyle: I did.
Mom: Then why are you still playing?
Kyle: I just wanted to finish this level real quickly.
Mom: Shut it off right now and get up to the bath!
Kyle: I can't shut it off!
Mom: What do you mean you can't shut it off?

Now I feel myself becoming angry!

Kyle: Because I have to save my game.
Mom: Then save it!
Kyle: I can't.
Mom: Why can't you?
Kyle: Because I have to finish this level before it will let me save.
Mom: How long will that take?
Kyle: Just a few minutes.

Mom: Well, hurry up, and then come upstairs.

Kyle: Okay, Mom.

Fifteen minutes later, no Kyle. Again, I find him in front of the game.

Mom: Kyle, I told you to save your game and get upstairs!

Kyle: I haven't saved my game yet!

Mom: You said it would only take a few minutes. Do it now!

Kyle: Okay, just a second.

All too aware that a "second" in video game time is much more than the tick of a clock, I demand immediate compliance—creating tension in the relationship. Exhausted by the frustration, I think about getting rid of Nintendo. But I don't, and the whole drama repeats itself the following evening.

Note to self: "It is hard work trying to restrict video game time!" Perhaps more than I care to endure.

I will never forget a conversation between Kyle and his Grandpa Otis during the early days of his Nintendo cravings. About eight years old at the time, Kyle slid next to Grandpa to inform him of his brewing plan.

"I'm going to ask my mommy if I can play Nintendo."

Aware of my rules on the subject, Grandpa asked Kyle, "What if she says no?"

"Then I'll keep asking and asking and asking until she says yes!" came Kyle's knowing reply.

Kids are hardwired with an intuitive understanding of how to push our buttons, manipulate our emotions, and overcome our resolve. And when it comes to video games, their motivation to play makes them push and push and push as hard as they need to in order to win!

The Slippery Slope

When it comes to video games, I am convinced that most parents will end up skidding down the proverbial slippery slope. We certainly did. Before we knew what happened or why, Kyle and our other children found themselves effectively negotiating away, discovering loopholes in, or skirting around, our rules restricting game time. In theory, they would be allowed only about two hours per week—and only as a reward for success in other areas. In reality, they spent more time than we cared to admit.

> When it comes to video games, most parents will end up skidding down the proverbial slippery slope.

Having already caved in, we came to accept video games as a necessary evil—the Looney Tunes and Brady Bunch of this generation. So we eventually allowed Kyle to trade in his hand-me-down system to purchase GameCube, the state-of-the-art system at the time. Once again, we rationalized the decision, telling ourselves that he was a good kid and successful student, that we would restrict his time and screen his games, and that it could be used to reward otherwise good choices. Like most parents, we accepted the status quo, running the yellow light of caution each of us felt in our gut.

Kurt began tapping the brakes before me. As had been the pattern of our parental partnership, I tended to wear the party hat while he played disciplinarian. On several occasions he nudged the issue, suggesting I had been too lenient when it came to game time. Even though the boys were doing their homework and chores, it bothered him to see video games consume so much playtime when there were so many other things they could be doing. Not wanting to admit what I knew to be an accurate assessment and hoping to avoid the conflict, I tried to find a middle ground.

"Video games are their first choice of what they want to do, and I get tired of saying no!"

By this time we had four children, including two preschool handfuls. In addition, my aging mother had been diagnosed with Parkinson's disease, and it fell upon me to manage her care. I had little energy to fight the restriction battle, thus giving the kids the upper hand.

"It is harder than you think," I would respond to Kurt's concerns. "Video games are their first choice of what they want to do, and I get tired of saying no!"

Sensitive to my stress, Kurt backed off, despite a gnawing sense that something unhealthful was happening to Kyle. As a result, I allowed him to slide further down the slope of an addictive path we didn't even know existed.

Decision Time

In December 2003 my mother's health took a dramatic turn for the worse. More of my time and energy went into her needs until she died from complications of the disease in March 2004. As you might imagine, those months were a blur: long stretches of time on the phone with doctors, nurses, and siblings; frequent visits to make sure Mom received proper attention at her home and with the doctors; borrowing babysitting favors from friends as I attempted to keep my head above water. I fell behind in every area of motherhood, including my role as video game monitor.

By the time I crawled out of a five-month season of intense stress and returned to normal motherhood, Kyle had grown accustomed to playing games more than I liked—a pattern that bled into summer break.

On the surface I had little reason for concern. After all, he was a great kid, spending at most two hours per day on GameCube. For the most part he still practiced his piano, read his books, completed his chores, even willingly took his baby sister to the park when asked. That summer I bought Kyle a thick science textbook to supplement what he would be learning at school the coming fall, and promised to purchase a new GameCube game for him when he finished the book. You'd never seen a kid more excited about reading a science text!

When Kyle was eight years old, it was somewhat cute watching his excitement at beating a game level. But I considered it a phase, something I hoped he would outgrow by the time he turned fourteen. As a matter of fact, I used to say to him, "When you go to high school, you won't have time to play video games anymore." Instead, I sensed a growing compulsion, with games dominating his thoughts and passions. I no longer considered it cute.

Why, I wondered, did I have this nagging concern? My son wasn't doing anything immoral or dangerous. Besides, I was more cautious than most parents, carefully screening and deciding which games the kids could play, making sure they completed other duties before powering up the system, limiting their playtime, and often leveraging games as a reward system by allowing them to earn minutes from time spent reading or playing board games. I knew parents who faced heartbreaking challenges with their kids, from failing grades to defiant rebellion to drug addiction. Was it silly to worry about a relatively minor issue like video games?

Silly or not, I did worry. Subtle at first, like the shadow of an approaching rain cloud, a growing concern grew in me that a dark, dampening influence was overtaking the sunshine of Kyle's youth.

I noticed a growing agitation in him. The more he played, the less he enjoyed other pursuits, as if he subconsciously resented anything that interfered with his singular desire. I sensed a loss of happiness, like someone had pulled the plug from the bottom of Kyle's joy tub and drained the cleansing refreshment of natural, healthy interests. He still did other activities, but with diminishing passion. When he read books, he did so hoping to trade chapters for more game time. Completing chores and playing with siblings became bargaining chips to play one more level. In short, given the choice, Kyle would pick video games over any other activity. In fact, when I specifically asked him why he always chose video games, he told me it was because "those other things are harder to do."

Shaun, our second boy, did not have the same reaction at first. For the most part, he could take or leave video games: he enjoyed them while he was playing, but was equally interested in other pursuits. Since he was two years younger than Kyle, I assumed age might have something to do with the difference. But then our seven-year-old, Troy, began joining the fun. Like a match to gasoline, Troy's interest quickly rivaled that of his oldest brother. What made these games so enticing to some children? More specifically, what was happening to my own kids? I knew something had to be done. But what?

Turning Point

Remembering my conversation with Julie from years earlier, I decided to seek her counsel once again. By this time, her son Jonathan had started law school after earning a quadruple major in college. I figured if anyone could put my mind at ease, it would be Julie, a mom who had effectively homeschooled a brilliant son and launched him into a successful college career while somehow managing his own draw toward video games. I just needed some comforting reassurance from Julie that everything would be fine—that video games were no big deal and that Kyle would outgrow this phase and become a successful, happy young man like Jonathan.

"Funny that you should call me this week," Julie began.

"Why is that?" I asked.

"Well, I had an interesting conversation with Jonathan while he was home from college. He said something I never expected to hear."

"What did he say?" I pressed.

"He told me he wishes I had taken video games away from him entirely when he was young." She paused to reflect. "But I remember him complaining about how much I restricted his time."

"Then why do you think he said that?"

"Because," she explained, "like many of his college buddies, he can't stop playing them now!" I could hear the regret in Julie's voice, as if she blamed herself for failing to prevent something she didn't know could happen. Like most of us, she had assumed that limiting the amount of time her son played would suffice. What she hadn't realized was that something far more serious than mere wasted time had been pulling Jonathan in a direction very difficult for any child to resist.

That conversation with Julie became a turning point. I knew I didn't want to receive a similar call from a grown-up Kyle and that making a tough decision now might avert downstream regrets. So I boxed up our game system and placed it in the closet until I could figure out the best course of action for our family.

Kyle grew anxious, wondering when his game system might return.

What I discovered made me wonder whether it ever should.

CHAPTER

2

MY PRECIOUS!

T
HOSE WHO HAVE read J. R. R. Tolkien's wonderful
The Lord of the Rings or seen the films will remember
a despicably pitiable character named Gollum. Unlike hobbits, with their simple pleasures and childlike charm,
Gollum lives in a perpetual state of dissatisfaction, driven
every waking moment by the desire to possess the magic ring
he affectionately calls "my precious!" After hundreds of years
of being enslaved to the ring's enticing lure, Gollum loses his
most prized possession. Tortured by withdrawal symptoms
far worse than those of a sickly, trembling junkie, Gollum
soon discovers that he, not the ring, is the one truly pos-
sessed.

In our home we began using the phrase "my precious" to
describe the effects Nintendo seemed to have on our boys'
ongoing attitudes and behavior, most notably their distressed

reaction to being told that game time was up. A joke, of course, but not far from the disturbing reality we discovered as we began to research the emotional, physiological, and social effects of video game addiction on kids.

In 2004 the *Washington Post* ran a story about the growing number of parents who find it necessary to enlist the help of therapists and support groups to deal with the problem.[1]

Sixteen-year-old Jaysen Perkins spent up to six hours per day playing the military role-playing game *SOCOM II*, performing missions with the U.S. Navy SEALs. But then it started undermining his social life and his grades. Jaysen's mom grew concerned about a month after her son started playing the game, when she noticed that he would get up in the middle of the night "trying to play any way he could."

The family sought help from Kim McDaniel, a licensed mental health counselor who treats about eight other game addicts at her private practice in Washington. McDaniel's patients are commonly six- and twelve-year-olds, both ages representing a transition into elementary or middle school and the struggle to relate to other kids. She frequently uncovers a connection to video game addiction and a correlating misunderstanding on the part of parents: "I often find that parents have nothing but the best intent with their children's relationship to technology, but there are a lot of myths out there."

One such myth is the notion that video games are engrossing but not addictive. McDaniel describes one of the reasons video games such as *Grand Theft Auto* and online games like *SOCOM II* and *EverQuest,* which allow multiple players to compete over the Internet, are potentially addictive—something manufacturers call the God effect. In more addictive role-playing games, players find themselves at the center of the universe, which McDaniel describes as very attractive for teens without a lot of power in the real world.

> Parents might wonder if their kids are getting into pot or cocaine, since the symptoms are similar.

Parents are advised to watch for two important signs in their children: withdrawal and isolation. Parents might wonder if their kids are getting into pot or cocaine, says Hilarie Cash of the Internet/Computer Addiction Services in Redmond, Washington, since the symptoms are similar.

For Jaysen Perkins, recognizing and addressing the problem has made a big difference. He has reentered the real world, attending his church youth group with friends and reclaiming old hobbies.

Californians Rick and Cynthia can relate. Their son Taylor felt the lure of "my precious" at six years old when they bought him his own Super Nintendo system in 1995. Concerned about the failure of his friends' parents to place limits on game choices and time, Rick and Cynthia decided to take control. "We decided to buy a system for our home so we could watch him," explains Rick. "He'd play all day if he could," adds Cynthia.

Maryanne, a National Geographic programming executive, has seen a similar pattern in her seventeen-year-old son, Kevin, that makes her cautious about the digital world, which she calls "a culture that they just slip into." She has seen her son stay up all night playing games on his video deck. When his grades slipped, she and her husband cut off access, then limited use to the post-homework hours. Kevin himself acknowledged that his gaming was getting out of hand when he started turning down invitations from friends to movies so that he could stay home and play video games.[2]

Similar patterns of game compulsion in my own children prompted me to ask whether there was something more there than childish irresponsibility, and several stories in the popular media reinforced my resolve to explore the issue further. A 1999 report from *Time Asia,* for example, asked the question "Is this stuff addictive?" citing psychologists who noted that players of video games showed symptoms similar to those induced by drugs and other pleasurable activities. UCLA psychiatrist Carole Lieberman says, "So the brain not only is seeing the images and getting stimulated, but it's also practicing a response. When the person is exposed to these violent media stimuli and it excites the psychoneurological receptors, it causes the person to feel this excitement, to feel a kind of high—and then to become addicted to whatever was giving him the high."[3]

This is no secret to game developers. While none of the companies *Time* contacted discussed the problem openly, one game developer shared anonymously that video games are all about the dynamics of adrenaline and that the easiest way to spike someone's adrenaline is to make him think he is going to die. He also discussed the Madison Avenue ad-agency principle at work in video games, the "blink rate": "People stop blinking if an ad has their attention. Same here—if you're into a game, your pupils dilate and your blink rate slows down." The article adds that this process produces dopamine, a neurotransmitter linked to addiction.[4]

> The easiest way to spike someone's adrenaline is to make him think he is going to die.

Long before my own children exhibited these patterns, BBC News in England ran a story, in November 2000, explaining that addiction is one of the chief criticisms leveled at video games. The charge suggests that they lead to compulsive behavior, diminished interest in other activities, association mainly with other "addicts," and the kinds of symptoms other addicts experience when denied their favorite pastime, such as "the shakes." The story describes characteristics of the individuals who succumbed to addiction.

A decade ago research showed that video game junkies were highly intelligent, motivated and achievement-oriented individuals. They did well in school and work. But could the more sophisticated games of the 21st Century be so all consuming as to interfere with that kind of achievement?

Dr. Mark Griffiths of Nottingham Trent University, an

expert on video game addiction, thinks it could just happen. "The video games of the 21st Century may in some ways be more psychologically rewarding than the 1980s games in that they require more complex skills, improved dexterity, and feature socially relevant topics and better graphics."

If these games offer greater "psychological rewards," players might be more at risk of developing an addiction, he said.[5]

The report goes on to describe some of the physical consequences of so much game time. What caught my attention, however, was Dr. Griffiths' list of questions that should trigger parental concern:

1. Does your child play almost every day?
2. Does your child often play for long periods (over three to four hours at a time)?
3. Does your child play for excitement?
4. Does your child get restless and irritable if he or she can't play?
5. Does your child sacrifice social and sporting activities to play?
6. Does your child play instead of doing homework?
7. Does your child try to cut down his or her playing but can't?

If the answer is "yes" to more than four of these questions, parents are told that they should be concerned. In our case we answered "yes" to four. But in addition, we found our son losing his capacity to enjoy other, more healthy activities like sports and board games. Therefore, I suggest adding an eighth question to Dr. Griffiths' list:

8. Does your child seem to be losing interest in real-life activities?

Research on video game addiction goes back more than twenty years, when digital games were not nearly as appealing and realistic as today's variety. Still, the results all point in the same direction: a growing risk to our children.

Similar to Substance Dependence

A November 2005 story in *New Scientist* magazine, titled "Gaming Fanatics Show Hallmarks of Drug Addiction," offers startling insight into just how similar video and computer game addiction is to more commonly understood addictions. Similar to chemical dependence, excessive video game play creates its own version of something called drug memories—visual cues in the brain that cause craving for the desired substance or activity.

> Similar to chemical dependence, excessive video game play creates its own version of something called drug memories.

Sabine Grüsser of the Charité University of Medicine, Berlin, conducted a study that showed how excessive computer game players exhibited classic signs of craving when presented with visual images from some of their favorite games. Those tested wanted desperately to play, expecting to feel better once they did, and fully intended to indulge again as soon as possible.[6]

Research presented at the 2005 Society for Neuroscience annual meeting in Washington, D.C., indicated that addictions stem from relying too heavily on one coping strategy, which eventually becomes the only activity that can activate the dopamine system and bring relief. "It's the same mechanism in all addicts," said Maressa Hecht Orzack, who founded a computer addiction service at McLean Hospital in Boston. What makes it tougher is that gamers cannot simply abstain from using computers, which are now an integral part of our lives. Therefore, Orzack suggests, the problem has to be approached in the same way that one would approach an eating disorder.

"Computer games have a reinforcing quality," agrees John Westland, a social worker at the Hospital for Sick Children in Toronto, Canada. "I don't think the comparison [to a drug of abuse] is a bad one."[7]

An earlier report titled "Measuring Problem Video Game Playing in Adolescents," released by the Society for the Study of Addiction to Alcohol and Other Drugs in 2002, compared the effects of video games to substance dependence.[8] The research focused on 223 adolescents in Spain, aged between thirteen and eighteen years, and classified as addicts those individuals who developed severe behavioral problems as a result of video game playing.

The study delved into some older research, including studies conducted in the early and mid-1980s that suggest up to 15 percent of those surveyed indicated signs of game addiction. In the 1990s researchers began borrowing methodologies used to measure a similar problem—pathological gambling. A 1995 study by Mark Griffiths and Imogen Dancaster showed that 8 percent of their sample were currently "addicted" to computer games, while nearly 30 percent were addicted at some time prior to the study. In 1998 Mark Griffiths and Nigel Hunt reported that one in five adolescents were addicted at the time of their study, with one in four having been addicted at some point in their lives.

So, nearly a decade ago one in four indicated "video game dependence." This suggests the likelihood of a much more serious problem today, in light of improved game graphics, in-depth story lines, and increased availability.

Having completed their summary of past research, the Society for the Study of Addiction report presented the methodology and findings of its own study. Criteria for substance dependence and for pathological gambling as well as the literature on addiction were reviewed in order to design a short scale for the measurement of problem video game playing.

Over 90 percent of the teens had played video games in the prior year, 57 percent at least once per week. Males were "significantly more likely" to play regularly than females (79 percent of males compared with 32 percent of females). The survey included the following statements for consideration:

- When I am not playing with video games, I keep thinking about them—i.e., remembering games, planning the next game, etc.
- I spend an increasing amount of time playing video games.
- I have tried to control, cut back, or stop playing, or I usually play with the video games over a longer period than I intended.
- When I lose in a game or I have not obtained the desired results, I need to play again to achieve my target.
- When I can't use the video games, I get restless or irritable.
- When I feel bad—e.g., nervous, sad, or angry—or when I have problems, I use the video games more often.
- Sometimes I conceal my video game playing from my parents, friends, teachers, etc.
- Because of the video game playing, I have reduced my homework or schoolwork, or I have not eaten, or I have gone to bed late, or I spent less time with my friends and family.

Video game "dependence" looks very much like other substance and behavioral addictions, most notably gambling.

Not surprisingly, commitment to video games was higher than that reported in early studies when games were less sophisticated and less prevalent.

So video game "dependence" looks very much like other substance and behavioral addictions, most notably gambling, with up to 25 percent of kids (boys more likely than girls at this point) becoming hooked.

Physiological Effects

Some of the most disturbing studies suggest a strong physiological response to playing video games and indicate clearly that game obsession is more than a behavioral problem. In one such study, doctors who allowed children to play video games on a Game Boy just prior to undergoing surgery found that the kids were more relaxed than if they had used tranquilizers or had held a parent's hand to keep them calm: "We find that the children are just so happy with the Game Boy that they actually do forget where they are," said Anu Patel, an anesthesiologist at University Hospital in Newark.[9]

According to David Sheff, author of the book *Game Over,* which chronicles the history and growth of the Nintendo phenomenon, hospital staff saw dramatic differences between playing video games and simply viewing television. Seriously ill children in a hospital who played Nintendo required half the pain medication as those who didn't. Television, in contrast, had no effect on the amount of medication required.[10]

Good news? Possibly. But if these "comfort" games replace the use of drugs when children undergo surgery, what does that suggest about their influence on a child's brains and emotions the rest of the time? Do we really want our children "sedated" on a daily basis?

In 1998 a report titled "Evidence for Straital Dopamine Release during a Video Game" published in the journal *Nature* describes a process called positron-emission tomography (PET). A team of British researchers found that video game playing actually changes the chemistry in the brain by increasing the activity of dopamine. Dopamine is one of the most important neurotransmitters in the brain, controlling movement, attention, and learning. As I mentioned earlier, it is also associated with reinforcement—triggered by events that produce pleasure—and with the reinforcing effects of addictive drugs like cocaine and amphetamines.

The subjects of the study were male volunteers aged thirty-six to forty-six. The game involved moving a tank through a battlefield on a screen, using a mouse. Subjects collected flags with the tank while destroying enemy tanks. If subjects collected enough flags, they progressed to the next game level. In other words, it used a pretty common video game template, involving battles, progressive challenges and rewards, and the opportunity to lose several lives. The study reported, "This task is comparable to tasks in animal studies in which dopamine is released during the anticipatory or appetitive phase of motivated behaviour, where dopamine is involved in learning which environmental stimuli or actions predict rewarding or aversive outcomes."[11]

Playing such games triggers reactions in the human brain similar to those observed among animals seeking food or water. Do you remember the research done by Russian physiologist Ivan Pavlov? At mealtime he rang a bell while serving food to his canine friends. After a while, ringing that bell caused the dogs to salivate no matter the time—even if they were not hungry. The pattern of reinforcement established in the brain remained independent of the desired object.

A similar process occurs in the brain when someone plays video games, creating an unconscious craving—a topic we will explore in a later chapter. For now, however, it is important to note just how strong the ringing bell of video games can be. Researchers at Hammersmith Hospital, a clinical research hospital in London, described the infusion of dopamine as being "similar to that observed following intravenous injection of amphetamine or methylphenidate."[12]

Using PET to scan the brain, these researchers found that dopamine levels were increased in a brain region called the striatum (an area known to be involved in the control of such movements as playing the piano) while subjects played a video game. A number of different components are recruited for playing video games, including attention, learning, and motor skills. It is entirely possible that any combination of these components could increase dopamine levels in the brain. Although brain imaging studies—including this one—can show us that a particular behavior produces a change in the brain, they can't tell us what it is about the behavior that is responsible for producing the change.

What about the reinforcing effects associated with playing video games? We know that many kids play video games for hours on end—their reinforcement being higher and higher scores.[13]

It should be noted that in this particular study researchers paid money for higher scores, which could have influenced some participants. Still, the clear message of the report is that playing video games releases a pleasure-inducing drug into the brain.

To put the research in layman's terms, kids who play video games submit their developing brains to a pleasurable chemical reaction similar to an amphetamine drug injection! And the more often they play, the more likely they are to become hooked on the feeling. No wonder they resist turning off the system, pleading instead for "just one more level."

Brain Train

In 2004 the National Institute on Media and the Family raised concerns about how video games may be shaping life-long appetites and character qualities in our teens:

> Advances in brain science show that children's experiences during their brain's growth spurts have a greater impact on their brain's wiring than at any other time of their lives. The groundbreaking discoveries about the teenage brain reveal that the growth spurts continue throughout adolescence, making teens more impressionable than we thought. Teenagers are wiring the circuits for self control, responsibility and relationships they will carry with them into adulthood. The latest brain research shows that violent games activate the anger center of

the teenage brain while dampening the brain's "con-
science."[14]

A growing number of parents find it troubling that video
games seem most prevalent during the season of life when
our children are being "hardwired" to become responsible or
idle, engaged or isolated, disciplined or lazy. Consider this
anonymous Web forum posting from one fed-up father:

> My son is a sophomore at Albany High, and he appears to
> be addicted to video games. I think his ideal life would be
> sitting in front of a computer monitor with an IV in his
> arm to deliver enough nutrients and caffeine that he
> wouldn't have to eat or sleep. He also has started to lie to
> his mother and me—and to his teachers—about his
> schoolwork to maximize his access to the video games,
> particularly those on the Web. He has some friends, but
> they tend to be limited to other "gamers." Does anyone
> have any advice and/or good resources for dealing with
> this problem? In one sense, I'm glad he isn't out on the
> streets getting into drugs or other forms of trouble. But I
> fear his life has become so one-dimensional that he will
> be damaged as a result of this obsession.

Every parent wants his or her kids to become happy,
healthy, productive adults. Unfortunately, a digital bell keeps
ringing in their ears, causing them to salivate on cue. And
there are no easy solutions, as the experiences of this concerned mom can attest:

We tried monitoring, reducing, limiting the hours he spent playing his favorite game. These were all just Band-Aids put on a serious injury and ultimately not successful. We recently took the game and threw it in the garbage. He was, surprisingly, not angry, and seemed almost relieved. I realize that this isn't a permanent solution, since computers are everywhere, but it's a start. I wish I had taken more aggressive action a long time ago, and I urge any parents facing this same situation to take it seriously.

"I wish I had taken more aggressive action a long time ago, and I urge any parents facing this same situation to take it seriously."

Some may feel that the word "addiction" is thrown around too lightly these days and that this is not a true addiction. I can testify from our experience that this is an addiction, and one that is not easily broken. It's not as easy as just finding other activities for your son to take part in. While they're in their gaming mode, they don't want to do anything else. That is inherent in the nature of an addiction . . . I certainly wish, for my son's sake, that I had known what I know now about this addiction.

Another parent on the forum tried to help his essentially good kid:

Computer overuse has been a serious problem for my seventeen-year-old for the past several years . . . My son plays online games and will play for twelve or fourteen hours straight, every single day, if no one objects, playing from the time he wakes up till he falls asleep in the early hours of the morning. He'll skip meals to play. He will wait till we have gone to bed and then play games till three or four in the morning every single night. Of course he cannot get up at 7 a.m. to go to school. He has never been very academically motivated, and the computer addiction greatly exacerbated the academic problem. He is no longer in school—he is waiting to take the high school equivalency exam. [Game playing] uses up all his time and keeps him from other activities like music and recreation. He is not writing computer programs or being otherwise creative. He is playing games for hours and hours on end. The only thing that works is physically removing the computer. We tried many other tactics. We'd say "computer after homework" but he'd say he had no homework. We tried taking away the computer till grades improved, and they'd improve, he'd get the computer back, and grades would take a nosedive again. We tried locking the keyboard in the trunk of our car (he found another keyboard), unplugging the Internet connection (he plugged it back after we went to bed), and taking out the graphics card (he borrowed one from a friend). So we have to take the CPU and lock it up. I feel like an ogre—I know how important e-mail and instant messaging are to teens and I really hate to take it away. I am myself a software engineer who's on the computer all day. I like games myself. But he is completely unable to limit the time he spends on games—it really is an addiction. Now he only gets his computer on the weekends, even though he is not in school anymore and has very little else to do. He complains continually and bitterly about this but even he agrees that he cannot control himself.

After listening to other parents, diving into the research, and facing a challenge with my own children, there is no doubt in my mind that computer and video games are highly addictive. But is it really all that serious? After all, our kids could be into drugs or some other illegal, immoral, or dangerous stuff.

In the next several chapters we will explore just how serious computer and video game addiction can be.

3

SADLY SUCCESSFUL

(TRUE CONFESSIONS)

ONE OF THE most enlightening and insightful interviews conducted during my research for this book was with Jonathan, the graduate student son of Julie, whom I introduced in chapter 1. As one who shares the fate of thousands of young men struggling with the compulsion to play games, twenty-three-year-old Jonathan gave me a chance to delve into the feelings and thoughts of a recovering video game addict who, despite being very successful, has many regrets.

I sat down with Jonathan at the local Starbucks. Jonathan's childhood education was a mix of public, private, and home schooling. He then went to college at the University of Colorado at Colorado Springs, got a BA and a BS in political science, philosophy, information systems, and international business, and is now in law school at Pepperdine.

Jonathan is an intelligent, hardworking young man. We started out the interview with him relating how he got into gaming.

> *Jonathan:* The first time I ever saw a Nintendo system was at my friend Paul's house, and I thought that it was very boring. I wasn't interested, didn't like it, but he was really into it, it was all he wanted to do, so I played with him some. I really grew to want one myself, just loved it, because whenever I went to his house, that's what we did. I was about six at the time. We played the original *Mario Bros.* game. It came out in about 1985, and man, it was a great game! So I asked my parents for one, again and again. They didn't think it was a good idea at first, but finally for Christmas they surprised me with it.

Jonathan went on to describe what he enjoyed about the games. As he spoke, I could see the excitement in his eyes as he recalled favorite childhood memories. He clearly loved his games, still does. We moved on to uncover how what started as a bit of innocent fun eventually took a huge bite out of life.

"I would read the magazine *Nintendo Power* when I wasn't allowed to play, look at all the maps, read the articles over and over again, wishing that I could play."

> *Jonathan:* The amount of time I played varied. My parents would restrict it, but I kind of knew it would only last a couple weeks, so I would put up

with it. Then for a while I could play only on weekends, but that went away too. I would read the magazine *Nintendo Power* when I wasn't allowed to play, look at all the maps, read the articles over and over again, wishing that I could play.

At one point my parents limited me to two hours a week, only on weekends. But that didn't last very long at all, and it got to the point that I would play eight hours on Sundays. I could have probably played more than eight hours a day. My friends would come over and they would play for a while, and then when they left, I'd just keep playing. My mom, to her credit, did not know I was playing so much, because at the time, the TV was upstairs in our "school room," rather than in the family room, which is where it was before, when they knew how much I was playing.

Jonathan shared that he had some kids bullying him at school and that the games seemed better to him than the real world. I had heard people compare games to other forms of entertainment that can provide escape from real life, such as movies or books. I asked if he saw a difference.

Jonathan: Well, I think the main and most powerful difference is that *you* are the character in a video game, particularly in role-playing games. You are the hero, and you're the one fighting the monsters, finding the keys and talking to people. Whereas with a movie or book, you read the story and you can become engaged in the story, but you're still an observer, not an actual participant. There's no sense of obligation at all. When you read the

Redwall series, you're thinking, "Ooh, what's Martin the Warrior going to do next?" But when you're playing a Nintendo game, it's "What am I going to do next, how do I get back, how do I beat this?"

I mean, think about it—do you want to leave this princess in captivity, or let this bad guy control the world? No, you've got to stop it. With books, you know what the ending is going to be. Maybe not exactly how it's going to happen, but you know the good guys are going to win. But there's a real element of uncertainty in video games that I think is very appealing. It depends on *you*, and *you* can save the world if you do well enough. You can fail and try again. But you can save the world. There is a strong sense of obligation. Who wouldn't want to save the world? With a movie there is no sense of obligation—and it's over in two hours, as opposed to fifty.

I wondered whether the heroic life Jonathan was living within his games made him more or less likely to emulate those heroic actions in real life.

Jonathan: Nintendo was to me more a world in itself. I wouldn't say it bled over very much, except when I couldn't play and that's what I wanted to be doing. I don't really even understand it now, much less back then at that age, but I can look back and see so many lost opportunities. The real world is so beautiful, but it's also such a tragic place, especially at a young age. It's hard to

"I look back and see so many lost opportunities."

perceive that we can make as big a difference in the world as we can in a game.

Jonathan was first exposed to Nintendo at age six and received his first game at about seven. I asked him to explain the process that led to his playing eight hours a day.

Jonathan: I think from the beginning I could have played that much. But I wasn't allowed. It wasn't until we moved the TV from the family room that I started doing heavy hours. I think that I put my world in boxes, like a lot of people do. I made excuses. "This is helping me to be a better person, I'm learning to be more heroic." I used to tell my parents that. My main excuses were that Nintendo helps people with hand-eye coordination and that it taught me how to be heroic. I could have gone outside and played basketball if hand-eye coordination was all I was truly interested in.

> "I could have played basketball if hand-eye coordination was all I was truly interested in."

I can't even imagine what it would have been like not to have the game. Nintendo was just such a huge part of my life. One thing that I think was a good substitute is board games, which I started playing in high school with a few guys. We would get together and play Risk and Samurai Swords, which is an eight-to-nine-hour board game. Unlike playing Nintendo, when you're playing a board game, you are focused on the game, but you're still talking about all kinds of stuff and laughing.

As far as bending the rules, or disobeying my parents,

I'll never forget one time in particular. I had made it to the first dungeon in the dark world in *The Legend of Zelda;* I shot the statue with a bow and arrow and the wall opened up, and there was a door right there, and Mom said, "You have to turn it off right now!"

Because I had been playing for an hour and a half, it was the time I was supposed to stop. But I couldn't believe it. I said, "No, I have to go in and see what this is and fall down through this new hole."

But she said, "No, turn it off." So I turned it off, and she said, "I'm going to the grocery store, and I don't want you to play this while I'm gone." I said okay, and she left. I ran upstairs, turned it on, and raced to that place as fast as I could. I made it there, and just as I was starting to go through the hole, I heard the garage door opening. I was scared to death. I turned it off, ran downstairs, with I'm sure a very guilty look on my face.

She asked me if I had played, and I lied. I was probably fourteen years old.

She said, "I saw the lights on in the window. I know you were playing."

After that, my parents said I couldn't play Nintendo for a month. I can look back on that and honestly say that was the hardest month that I can remember in my first eighteen years. It was hard because I wanted to be playing all the time, and it was all I thought of. I honestly could not imagine not playing for a month, especially with that door still there.

I asked Jonathan to share his thoughts about addiction, making the comparison to alcohol. Early on, every alcoholic can say no to alcohol. But they eventually reach a point where the bottle is controlling them rather than the other way around. If at fourteen years old Jonathan had the worst month of his eighteen years simply because he couldn't play video games, was that an indication that he was addicted?

Jonathan: Well, I think it depends on what definition you use for addiction. If you mean did it control my thoughts, my actions, and my desires? Then yes, 100 percent, I was addicted, I freely admit it. If by addiction one means I had absolutely no power to stop, that I had no choice in the matter, I don't think that anyone is truly addicted in that sense.

I still struggle as an adult. This whole last semester I have fought against it. I mean, I'm in London, I shouldn't be playing video games, and I should be going to museums and stuff. But I took a game with me for some reason, I don't know why.

I probably should be trying to go cold turkey. But this last Sunday I thought, "You know what? I'm so tired; I think I'm going to take a break and play, just for a little while." I sat down at about five in the evening and started playing, and I'd beaten this game before, of course. I wound up playing until after midnight, until I could beat it again. Afterward, I thought, "Man! I thought I was over that, just sitting down and playing for seven hours." It kind of reinforced the idea that yes, this is something I still definitely need to be working on, just like a recovering alcoholic. I mean, you can't, I would imagine, take just one drink.

I asked Jonathan what advice he would offer a mother who has a child similar to himself who says, "My child thinks about video games all the time."

Jonathan: Get rid of it, completely, entirely. I wish my mom had done that. Even if you limit the actual playing time, you're not going to eliminate the kids thinking about it as long as it's in the house. Even though I wasn't allowed to play for a month, it was still all I thought about. So if you're allowed to play fifteen minutes a week, for me that still would have occupied a huge majority of my time: thinking about it, wanting to do it, etc. I can't tell parents what to do, but I would encourage them to think very carefully about whether or not they have the ability, one, to know that their children will be able to handle it and, two, to enforce boundaries that are put in place.

"When my parents put restrictions on game time, I pushed them very hard."

When my parents put restrictions on it, I pushed them very hard, saying, "Can I please go ahead? It's a special day because of this or that," or, "I had a really good day in math today." So as a reward I would get to play Nintendo for a while.

There is a time, I think, when a parent should say no completely. Don't ask, "Are video games okay?" but rather, "Is this the best use of time and money?" In my experience the answer to that is often no. Also, you might ask, "What can we be doing together as a family?"

When I sit down to play games, if I thought about it, I might realize, "There has to be something better that I can be doing with my time." Yes, it's good to have downtime, but there are so many activities to participate in other than video games. For me, the costs of games outweigh the benefits. And I think for a lot of people, if you look at it objectively, you might have to say that's the case.

When parents take video games away from kids, they feel like they are being too strict, overprotective, etc. I wondered whether Jonathan would say it is worth the battle.

Jonathan: Number one, it's the parents' responsibility to raise the children . . . I guarantee your child is not going to be happy about it. I would have not been happy about it for months probably. But I don't think it's the children's decision how the house is run. If parents honestly do believe it shouldn't be in the house, it's irrelevant whether or not the kids are going to be upset, because if [the parents] are doing it for the kids' good in the long run, it's worth a little bit of pain now. And certainly worth the joy that will come later because of that choice.

By the time a child goes to college, everyone has a system, so it really becomes a nonissue, like, "Oh, I can't have it? Fine, I'll just go to one of the six other people on this floor and play it there." Once someone has moved out of the house, they're making their own choices. You can try to influence them—like with my sister, we have a deal where neither one of us drinks alcohol—but we can't enforce those choices, because she's in Baltimore and I'm not. She can take my advice, or my parents' advice, or she can choose not to. In law school the girls don't have systems. But in the guys' dorm every night, and this is one of the things I had a hard time with, there is someone playing somewhere all the time.

Looking back over twenty-three years of life, would Jonathan say, on the whole, that video games have generated more joy in his life or less?

Jonathan: In general, I would say less because of the sense of discontent that the video games breed. You want to play them all the time, and even when you're playing, in reaching achievements you have to work very hard and long to get there. But by and large, I look back and see myself as happy some of the times, but not really joyful. I think there is incredible potential for real joy in the world without having to look for happiness in video games.

I'm not surprised when I hear of marriages falling apart because of a husband's game addiction, especially in light of the online games that are available today. There are teams of people at the software firms creating new scenarios, and you're online with hundreds of thousands of people.

It's kind of like alcoholism; now I kind of try to stay away from the bars! I know there are hundreds of thousands of people who play these games online nowadays, but I have made a conscious effort to not get into those.

If Jonathan were to create a list of signs to help parents determine whether or not their child has a propensity for video game addiction, what would he include?

Jonathan: If they're playing Game Boy in the car all the time. If they are coming home and sitting down to play video games. If they are preferring their video games over being with people, that is a problem. If they're putting video games over their homework, over their responsibilities, that's a problem. If their friends are coming over and leaving and the child is still playing video games, I think that's a problem. If other kids in the same situations are getting tired of this and walking away, and the one child still wants to play, with the attitude "I will play for as long as I'm allowed," that indicates a problem.

I would stop to eat, and then I would go start playing again. I think in college there were times I'd play for five or six hours and I would stop, mostly because it was late at night and I needed to go to sleep.

I never stopped just because I got bored with the games. There are always new games. There were a few times where I would think, "I'm tired of all these, 'cause I've beaten them all so many times. Now, which one should I beat again?"

I think the real question is not whether kids will be able to maintain their grades, but are they able to meet their potential? Again, how are they using their time, and if they're wasting this much time, what more could they be doing? To say, "They're getting everything done, so I guess it's okay if they waste five hours a day on gaming," I don't think that's the right attitude. One thing that was a huge shocker for me was when I realized in law school— it took me until law school to realize this because grades did come a little easier for me in college—that in real life you don't get to start over. It may sound goofy, but when you're playing games, if you make a mistake, it's okay, there's very little risk involved. All of a sudden, when I didn't do as well as I wanted to in my first semester, it was like, "Wow, that was a one-shot deal!" And I think that a lot of times it's hard to realize that life is a one-shot deal, when you play games so much.

I've often heard adults dismiss the harmful influence of video games on children because they observe kids like Jonathan who show few obvious symptoms of addiction. After all, Jonathan continued to get good grades, finish his chores, and succeed in his work. The insights he shared with me, however, reveal a problem that may never trigger a caution light on many parental dashboards. As Jonathan's experience shows, it is difficult to measure the impact that years of discontent and lost potential can have.

CHAPTER

4

MADE FOR ADDICTION

OVER THE PAST decade we have witnessed grow-ing hostility against the tobacco industry, due to increased awareness of health hazards and the ad-dictive nature of nicotine. Class-action lawsuit settlements and dramatically higher cigarette taxes continue to drive the price of cigarettes through the roof. Smoke-free zones now dominate the airline and restaurant industries and many workplaces, causing smokers to feel like second-class citizens throughout much of the nation.

Do you remember the public outcry when Camel launched its "Joe Cool" cigarette marketing campaign be-cause it targeted young people? Parents, educators, and health officials were outraged that a multibillion-dollar in-dustry would market a highly addictive product to children despite the harmful effects. If those same folks understood what is happening within the video game industry, they would issue a similar outcry.

Driving Forces of Game Addiction

Like nicotine in cigarettes, certain aspects of popular games are intentionally designed to ensure their addictive appeal. Several game design Web forums offer advice on how to build into games "driving forces" of addiction.[1] I have attempted to summarize and simplify the key elements I have discovered.

> Like nicotine in cigarettes, certain aspects of popular games are intentionally designed to ensure their addictive appeal.

Driving Force 1: Beating the Game

The first driving force for game addiction is the desire to finish, in part due to the satisfaction of completion or simple pride—wanting to beat the game. By allowing players to compete against the system itself, rather than other players, video games possess an addictive draw not found in sports, board games, and other more interactive activities. Of particular concern are single-player games that can encourage long periods of isolation.

Driving Force 2: Competition

Everyone loves to compete, especially boys. Competition is a cornerstone of video and computer games. Allowing people to interact with each other puts the game in the hands of the players, rather than the game programmer. Players figure out their own traps and snares for each other, going beyond anything the developer could have conceived. Creating a game with flexible rules allows players to develop their own playing styles, moves, and tactics. In addition to beating a predesigned game template, they compete against an infinite variety of possibilities brought to the game by other players.

Driving Force 3: Mastery

The desire to master a game is also potentially addictive. Automobile or aircraft simulations, for example, give the player control of a particular vehicle. Unlike story-driven games, players will go back and start over in order to improve and refine their skills. The design trick for such games is to create detail levels in the controls. In a driving game a simple turn can be made more exciting and challenging by allowing players to feel the road and give when the tires lose traction, such as a sound signifying the tires beginning to lose traction or the sound of the engine in different gears while pushing through a turn. Anything the players can use as a map to understand how the game is functioning will draw them to want to master it. Programmers are encouraged to give players enough "feedback" from the game so that they can learn to master it, drawing them back over and over again.

Driving Force 4: Exploration

The addiction of exploration has been part of computer games since the beginning. In fact, some of the first games were entirely about exploration. The wildly popular game *Myst,* for example, used exploration as its basis, capitalizing on the strong urge to explore interesting places or uncover secret levels. From *Super Mario Bros.* to *Final Fantasy VII* a key facet of addiction has been discovering secret levels. Some designers suggest that 40 percent of a video game's levels should be hidden. The driving force for players, of course, is to solve the mystery—be it finding the hidden levels or learning game secrets and feeling like they are left hanging until they can get back to the game to do so.

Driving Force 5: The High Score

Achieving or beating a high score falls within two categories of addiction but is important enough to list as its own driving force. Normally, someone who is trying to get a high score in a computer game is either trying to compete against another player's score or trying to master the game. Players spend countless hours playing video games simply to beat a competitor's high score—even if that "competitor" is one's own last game! It happened with early pinball games and continues in the escalating ladders of today's Internet games. Another type of high-score addiction is completing rather than just beating the game. Think of it as walking through one hallway door and defeating the nemesis, but then realizing there are many other doors to open before you have "completed" the game.

Driving Force 6: Story-Driven Role Play

Successful game programmers tap another powerful ally in addiction—story motivation. Designing the game to the script of a story will compel players to finish, to see how the story ends. Even many of the games designed for younger children work from a simple story line, pushing players because they want to beat the game to rescue the princess, capture the prize, etc.

Most games allow you to control the actions of an on-screen character. Many, however, go much further by letting the player become a character in the story, thus creating a strong sense of obligation to continue play. Such role-playing elements of video games tend to draw a child back repeatedly, in part because the child has adopted a temporary replacement identity and feels responsible for continuing the narrative—in other words, the outcome "depends on me." The harder it is to finish the quest or story, the more likely the game will feed addiction. This is why more and more games are designed with a story foundation and with increased level complexity.

Driving Force 7: Relationships

Many video and Internet games are designed to create an odd type of peer pressure in which players rely upon each other for support. Gamers also play for long periods of time to improve their character's skill and attributes in order to stay on par with others. If one does not advance from one level to the next quickly enough, he or she falls behind the pack, risking getting kicked out of the unit.

Such games also leverage the draw of artificial relationships, allowing players to build "friendships" with people they would not otherwise meet or even like. Thanks to anonymity, people feel more open talking about personal issues online without fear of judgments they might face from real-life friends and family. Marissa Reedhead, for example, describes herself as a short, overweight brunette. "I'm not judged by the way I look when I'm online," says Reedhead, a twenty-four-year-old teacher in Thunder Bay, Ontario, who's been playing *The Sims* for three years. "I'm well-spoken and intelligent and these are the things people see when they're talking to me."[2]

WHEN YOU COMBINE these "driving forces" intentionally designed into video games with the influx of dopamine triggered during play, you have a potent combination feeding the addictive impulse.

An episode of *The Jane Pauley Show* in 2005 featured a twenty-two-year-old college student named Kenneth who was addicted to video games. During the show a medical professional tested the physiological effects of Kenneth at play. In the few moments of anticipation preceding play, the young man's blood pressure rose significantly. His heart rate, which began at 85 beats per minute, increased 40 percent within about five minutes of play. After twenty minutes of play the young man's heart rate increased to 155. Ten minutes later it peaked at 190—classified as extreme hypertension.

The attending medical professional observed that an individual's heartbeat and blood pressure will rise at a similar pace with physical exercise. The increase during video game play, however, is very different because it is a behavioral stressor. Those addicted to video games, he explained, over time must play more and more in order to achieve the same level of arousal.[3]

> Those addicted to video games over time must play more and more in order to achieve the same level of arousal.

Understanding Addiction

When I speak about video game addiction, I'm often asked a very good question. "But you can become addicted to anything, can't you?" Many parents, myself included, would prefer to lump video games in with other activities that can get out of control if left unchecked, including television, reading, or sports. We all know, however, that some addictions can be more dangerous and enticing than others. That is why it is important for us to examine the nature of addiction itself, including what happens to the brain.

While I am by no means an expert on the topic, I have gleaned very helpful insights from those who are. Most notably, Gerald G. May, MD, who is the author of *Addiction and Grace*, among the best books available for lay readers hoping to understand the patterns and prevention of addiction. I encourage every parent to read Dr. May's book to gain a better perspective on these matters.[4]

Dr. May describes a progressive process that occurs in the brain leading to addiction. He compares it to three stairsteps descending into slavery.

Step One: Feedback

When we encounter stress, the cells in our brains kick into self-defense mode. Feedback has been called the first line of that defense, an initial reaction against imbalance in the brain. One of three things occurs: overactive cells are inhibited, underactive cells are stimulated, or cells functioning well may be facilitated. If, for example, I stub my toe while walking, stress occurs. Spinal cord cells almost instantly cause a reflex. At the same moment, thousands of other cells further up my spinal cord respond to the sensation of pain by sending an alarm message to my brain demanding a response. Left to themselves, those same cells in my spinal cord could overreact to the situation. So in order to restore equilibrium and enable an appropriate response, my brain will send inhibiting messages back—in essence telling those cells to calm down. The end result is for me to hold my foot and cry "ouch" rather than become a crazed maniac in reaction to a minor stress.

Dr. May explains that most feedback that naturally occurs in the brain is inhibitory. Like two people in conversation, one telling the other to calm down and speak more slowly when overexcited, inhibitory feedback works to restore the normal balance of cell dialogue. If that initial feedback does not work, however, or if it must be repeated over and over, the person will experience even more stress because the body will do whatever it must to quiet the source of stress. At this point the second step in the process of self-defense has begun.[5]

Step Two: Habituation

In prolonged stress situations nerve cells become less sensitive and responsive to whatever stimuli are sending messages to the brain. Cells can actually inhibit their own receptors and actively suppress the transmission of incoming impulses. The brain cells no longer simply ask the nerve cells to speak softly. They actually tape their mouths shut by restricting conduction of impulses. This process can be good. It allows us, for example, to become unaware of background noises so that we can concentrate. But the effort required by the brain cells to suppress unwanted stimuli for long periods of time can be exhausting, depleting neurotransmitters and energy sources. So a long-term solution kicks in. Nerve cells begin to undergo actual physical changes, destroying their own neuroreceptors and severing their synaptic connections with the sending cells. Such "habituation" occurs in order to protect equilibrium in the larger system.

When neither feedback nor habituation is enough to restore balance, however, a new balance must be created through a process called adaptation.

Step Three: Adaptation

Eventually, the brain will say, "If you can't beat them, join them." Adaptation is the brain's way of joining in rather than tuning out. Rather than remain in a prolonged state of imbalance or stress, the system must adapt to a new normality. As Dr. May explains: "Adaptations occur through physical changes in the cells of the nervous system: synapses formed and dissolved, connections established and broken, neurotransmitters changed in kind and amount, neuroreceptors altered in number and responsiveness. Adapting to change, then, means going through the stress of withdrawal from the old normality and finding relief when a new normality is established."[6]

While we resist leaving behind the old "normal" in order to accept the new, we must eventually accept reality, pack up, and move on. This process, also called attachment, makes human beings the most adaptable creatures in God's creation. That is the good news. But there is also bad news. This very capacity to create new normalities in search of stress relief also makes us vulnerable to countless attachments. With each, a new addiction can emerge.

THE THREE-STEP process of feedback, habituation, and adaptation can occur in children triggered by the stress of video game play. Trying to protect itself from prolonged intensity, agitation, or even excitement, the brain eventually accepts the new normality and "attaches" the child to a world of virtual play. Rather than the abnormal exception, video games become the brain's expected routine—a pattern intensified by the infusion of dopamine explained in chapter 2.

"Regardless of how an addiction begins," writes Dr. May, "the longer it lasts the more powerful it becomes. Attachments are thus like spreading malignancies, steadily invading and incorporating their surroundings into themselves." Addictions have been aptly compared to "greedy dogs, never satisfied," and to an appetite "as insatiable as death."[7]

I suppose you could say that human beings, including our children, are actually hardwired for addiction, because the same mechanism that is designed to help us adapt to changing environments can be hijacked for attachment.

As a Christian, Dr. May believes, as I do, that we are made for relationship with our Creator. Part of the package includes the gift of freedom, allowing us to choose between what is good for us and what is not. All of us, therefore, have the option to foster a healthful desire for things that bring joy or an unhealthful compulsion for things that can enslave through addiction. When the latter happens, says May, a process begins that moves us further and further away from that for which we were made.

> Psychologically, addiction uses up desire. It is like a psychic malignancy, sucking our life energy into specific obsessions and compulsions, leaving less and less energy available for other people and other pursuits. Spiritually, addiction is a deep-seated form of idolatry. The objects of our addictions become our gods. These are what we worship, what we attend to, where we give our time and energy, instead of love. Addiction, then, displaces and

supplants God's love as the source and object of our deepest true desire. It is, as one modern spiritual writer has called it, a "counterfeit of religious presence."

Addiction exists wherever persons are internally compelled to give energy to things that are not their true desires. To define it directly, addiction is the state of compulsion, obsession, or preoccupation that enslaves a person's will and desire. Addiction sidetracks and eclipses the energy of our deepest, truest desire for love and goodness. We succumb because the energy of our desire becomes attached, nailed, to specific behaviors, objects, or people. Attachment, then, is the process that enslaves desire and creates the state of addiction.[8]

I clearly observed this addictive process taking hold in my son's situation as his energy and desire for what is good, healthful, and natural gradually became displaced by an obsession to play video games. He, like so many, found the empty thrill of virtual pursuits replacing the kind of deep satisfaction and enjoyment that can come from the real world.

Distraction or Replacement?

According to a 2005 study conducted by the Kaiser Family Foundation on the media consumption habits of children aged eight to eighteen, time staring at a television screen eclipses time spent playing video games by about 300 percent.[9] Doesn't this suggest that video games, while a problem, are less troublesome than television? In terms of wasted time, certainly. But when it comes to the question of addiction, in my view video games fall into an entirely different category.

Watching television is a passive activity. It serves as a *distraction* from real life. Playing video games, by contrast, requires full participation. Rather than a distraction, it becomes a *replacement* for real life. The child enters a virtual world and becomes the character. With reading a book or watching television, the child *observes* characters in a story. With video games, the child *becomes* the character and feels an obligation to succeed. Because this obligation pulls the child further into a virtual existence, it pulls him away from real satisfaction. To use Dr. May's words, it sucks life energy into a virtual obsession, leaving less and less energy available for natural pursuits.

> With reading a book or watching television, the child *observes* characters in a story. With video games, the child *becomes* the character and feels an obligation to succeed.

When children become addicted to video games, they experience a gradual process of acquiring a taste for emotional and spiritual poison—but not because the content of games is necessarily evil. In fact, the themes of many are pretty harmless. Instead, it is because these children are moving down a path that C. S. Lewis described as "an ever increasing desire for an ever diminishing satisfaction." The more pleasure they get from playing games, the less joy they experience overall.

The Kaiser Family Foundation study reported that those children who are least content or get the poorest grades spend more time with video games (about an hour per day) and less time reading than their peers. They observed no similar correlation with television viewing.

My great concern for my son was not that playing video games would turn him into an evil person, despite a clear tendency toward increased agitation, discontent, and unrest. My concern was that he would become a less joyful person with diminished capacity to drink in the beauty, excitement, and passion of real life.

Author Mark Rutland provides great insight into what happens when we, or our children, descend into such attachments. His book *Behind the Glittering Mask* is not about video games, but rather about those things that steal joy and purpose from life, including the "deadly sin" of sloth. In a debate between Lucifer and Michael the archangel, Rutland describes what happens to those who lose the passion of real life due to cheap imitations: "Sloth creates a culture reaching for the mirage of success without work." It also "recreates culture in the image of society's least creative, least beautiful, least productive, and least disciplined. The art of Sloth is bastardized by the idolatry of Sloth which is ease."[10]

Video games create the illusion of manhood for boys and young men by simulating heroic conquest through masculine pursuits and rewards without any of the risk and danger of real heroism. One young man I interviewed shared that in the virtual world he was a conquering hero. In the real world, however, he was a lazy bum wasting his time and life. As Rutland describes, the slothful abort their own lives "because they will not suffer the pain, pay the price, exert the effort, or endure the wait that would have allowed them to grow . . . They live weary, puny lives, constantly waiting for the unfulfilled pipe dream, the ship that never comes in, and the gamble that never pays off. They descend by the steps of 'get rich quick schemes' into the basement of poverty."[11]

Video games create the illusion of manhood for boys and young men by simulating heroic conquest through masculine pursuits and rewards without any of the risk and danger of real heroism.

If observing such patterns overtake one's child is not bad enough, imagine how I felt reading Rutland's description of how parental sloth contributes to this deadly sin's grip on children: "Parenting shrivels because it takes discipline to lovingly train another. It is easier to indulge a child than to shape his character. 'Giving in' is the path of least resistance, least effort, and least love. Chastening, teaching, rebuking, and even properly punishing a child takes time, perseverance, and sacrifice. To give him what he pleads and weeps and screams for costs very little."[12]

Ouch! My own slothful approach to parenting in this arena—giving in to what I thought would make my son happy—actually pushed him further away from joy. That is one of the main reasons I felt compelled to write this book: to provide other moms and dads with information I wish I had known before making such an unintended mistake.

5

LOST POTENTIAL
(TRUE CONFESSIONS)

O NE OF THE serious problems uncovered during my research for this book is the alarming number of young men who, unlike "straight A" Jonathan from chapter 3, are literally flunking out of college due to game addiction. Sadly, many of their parents managed the amount and type of game play while these boys were growing up—only to find them sucked into the vortex of a gaming culture that is overtaking college dorm life.

I sat down with Steve, a twenty-three-year-old college student who found it necessary to hit the restart button on achieving his life goals after flunking his sophomore year due to excessive video game play. We began by discussing the relatively limited game influence in Steve's early experience.

Steve: I got started playing video games when I was about eleven or twelve. I convinced my mom to buy our first video game system. At the time, she was kind of hesitant, so she put a lot of stipulations on it, how often we could play, what games we could play. She was pretty good about it. We couldn't play any violent games or anything like that. They really didn't have rating systems then, so she would view the content of the game and make her decisions from that.

I was mainly into sports games when I was little. The only reason I really wanted to have it was to play sports games. We had some little kids' role-playing games too, like *Super Mario* and *Hedgehog*. When we first got it, we played a lot of Disney games, like *The Lion King*, things that went along with the movies. That was my first experience. Some of my friends had more of the frightening games, like *Mortal Kombat*. My mom wouldn't let me play it, so, of course, I really got a kick out of it. I don't know if she knew or not. During the school year in middle school, she restricted video games, just like she did TV. Then in the summertime I remember playing a lot of video games, like when we'd go on family vacations.

Looking back, there were times that I would get into a video game, and instead of doing my homework, I would stay up late playing a video game. I'd go to school tired. With a couple of the games, like when *James Bond* first came out, some of my friends and I would skip class and go to a friend's house and play games. In that way you could say that it affected my grades as a kid.

I wasn't really into school during high school. Whether

I withdrew from school to play games or played games because I didn't care about school, I can't say. Overall, I felt I kept video games under control. It wasn't something I "had" to do. Most teenagers don't want to be in the house with their parents. I just kind of avoided them, killing time with a game. So at the house, games were an escape from whatever was going on. Playing with my friends, on the other hand, was a more social thing.

When I got to college, the "social thing" continued. I was in a suite with two other guys and we had a lot of guys on our floor. Everyone played different kinds of video game—on the computer, PlayStation, or whatever. Everyone's getting to know each other, playing football video games. It slowly progressed from there. If you didn't want to do your homework or study, and you were looking for a reason, this was right in front of you. You'd forget how much time you spent playing.

I saw a lot of extreme cases at school. You could tell which kids were really into video games and were just kind of absent from life. Games were their only source of enjoyment. I'm one who definitely played too much, even for my own comfort.

I remember my freshman year in the dorm, this new game came out. I had to have it; I went and got it. It was a role-playing game and it never ended. It just went on and on. I played it for a week, and it ate up all my free time. Everyone would come over to our dorm at night and play video games or sports games. All of a sudden I was enveloped in it. It was everywhere.

All we did was play video games. It was really weird. I

didn't want to get into it because I knew I would be selling myself short by spending so much time doing it. I knew how it affected me, but it was something I couldn't really control. I'd try to set a time limit, like I'd say I'm going to bed at eleven, but it always seemed difficult to do and I'd end up going to bed at like two in the morning. You know it's not going to end up fulfilling you; you don't really want to do it but end up doing it anyway.

> "You know it's not going to end up fulfilling you; you don't really want to do it but end up doing it anyway."

I've asked several young men, "Did you ever play when you didn't want to be playing?" Every one of them said yes. Steve was no different.

Steve: There would be times when we would stay up all night long. When I was with friends, it was sometimes easier to put the controller down and go to bed than when I was into a game by myself. I began playing more role-playing games by myself, because they're no fun to play with people sitting around. By myself I'd play for hours. When you're playing with friends, it's usually some kind of competitive game, and it just gets old after a while.

I think what made it hard is that I was never really positive that it was the games causing my life to be out of whack. I just felt it was something inside of me. Whether it was tied to my self-esteem or sense of purpose, something was out of whack and it just manifested itself in my playing video games.

There are times when being a college student can be overwhelming. By turning to video games so much, you really do lose self-esteem and confidence that you can face adversities in life and be successful. It is a very vicious cycle. When you don't succeed or live up to your expectations, all of a sudden it's reinforcing the cycle because you go back to the video games to escape your sense of failure. It's just easier.

My freshman year I lived in the dorms, and I did really badly in school. When I came back to school in my sophomore year, I lived in a house with two other guys. I was really committed to getting back on track and working hard. I thought that a lot of the problems I had—playing video games, my sleep cycle, and my overall health—were problems because I lived in the dorms, around so many people who played all the time. I thought just living with two other guys would end that, but it didn't. One of the guys went out and bought a big-screen TV, and that's what we did when we weren't in class, which was most of the time. We were in front of the TV, either watching it or playing video games. It caught up with me, and I couldn't get rid of the problem. I ended up failing out of school that first semester of my sophomore year. I started off that semester on probation and I failed out of school. I moved down to my dad's house in Albuquerque, where I am right now. When I came down here, I said, "Okay, that's it," and I got rid of the video games. It was really easier to do once I was by myself. I decided I was going to get my life back on track.

I spent a year working full-time, and then I moved back to Colorado and started school again. I started hanging out with friends again, a lot of whom played video games. But it wasn't something that sucked me in this time, thanks to the habits I formed during that year.

I had a completely different attitude and work ethic. I think for the first time, I really valued my time. And if I value my time, I'm not going to sit around playing video games. I'd think of all the other things I could be learning and doing and accomplishing with my life—and those things were not going to happen if I was playing video games.

> "I'd think of all the other things I could be learning and doing and accomplishing with my life—and those things were not going to happen if I was playing video games."

It's kind of interesting, because even after video games had been completely cut out of my life, there were times when I went home and played with my brother, who had a system. Because I went home to rest and relax, I really didn't have any commitments to myself. So I noticed that the video games would kind of sneak up, and before I knew it, I would be playing them more than I liked.

I transferred to Denver University and began living in the dorms again. I was in a suite with six people. Only one of my roommates played video games. It was interesting how the five of us who didn't play were so productive. The one guy who did play, played like those games were his life. It was really sad to see that extreme, to see how the games dominated his life. He went through two or three different roommates that couldn't live with him because he'd stay up all night playing whatever it was that he was playing.

I lived in the dorms for two quarters, then I had to take some time off school for financial reasons. I stayed in Denver for a little while before I came down to my dad's house. I moved in with my brother-in-law's two brothers, Josh and Brian, who lived with two other guys. It was really frustrating for me to live in that household and in that environment, because all they did was play video games or computer games. They had everything set up in the basement. It seemed almost like I avoided them completely, because they were always in the basement and I didn't want to be anywhere around that. So I stayed upstairs.

The times I would stray down to talk to them, somebody would say, "Hey, let's play a game." A couple times I found myself playing longer than I wanted to play even though I had to go to work in the morning. When that happened, I got really frustrated that I didn't have the discipline to walk away when I said I was going to walk away. I knew the kind of repercussions it was going to have, whether it was being tired at work or not doing my best schoolwork or whatever. It really frustrated me. I tried to make that a strong point, that I was not going to let this happen again, and I've been pretty successful. I'm not going to let them talk me into playing video games until two in the morning.

I've noticed that in my own environment, with things that I control, I try to get rid of distractions like that completely. But when it's in an environment that I can't control, like at my brother's house, I really have to make sure that I step back and say, "How am I going to spend my time while I'm here?" I have to have something productive to do, whether it's reading or writing or just anything that increases my self-worth. If I don't, that's when it's very easy to get hooked again.

Parents fear that getting rid of their children's systems might be considered too radical. Obviously, all video games are not evil. But many parents don't want to take the risk of allowing game systems in their child's life, in light of their addictive nature. I asked Steve to share his opinion.

Steve: I think that's a very fine line and a hard stand to take. And it's not just video games, but so many things that are available to children today with technology and stuff. It's like, "How do I let my children enjoy this without pacifying him or her?" So I think parents really need to take a hands-on approach with their children, to teach them how to become strong individuals, teach them some values, to value yourself and value others.

It's so easy for parents nowadays to just pacify their children instead of really putting their time and effort into it. When their children say they're bored or they're crying or whining, parents give their children the TV or videos. I definitely think parents need to be involved and make those decisions with them.

Another thing parents can do is set very clearly defined time limits. Parents might have to take the controllers and keep them in their possession until it's time to play. The game provides so much stimulation. When you're playing it, you are rewarded with all of this gratification. I think it's something that needs to be limited. It can't just be accessed whenever that desire kicks in.

I think mainly parents just need to be involved in their kids' lives, whether it's through family activities or sports or whatever. They need to talk to their children more. They come home from work to the whining and fussing of their kids, and too many parents just pawn off video games or other technology on their kids to keep them out of their hair.

It really stems from parents wanting their children to be happy. I don't think that's a realistic approach to life.

I was talking to my stepmother and my dad the other day about the difference between growing up in my generation and their generation. When they grew up, they were kind of expected to suffer. My family took road trips, and they were so boring. The only way to avoid the boredom was to read, or my mom would play *Adventures in Odyssey* tapes. I give my mom a lot of credit; she was always trying to stimulate us with other games and stuff, to help us grow educationally and as a person. Now, with all these cars with the DVD players in them, the kids don't have to be bored. They're automatically pacified and I think it's setting them up for failure because it teaches them they don't have to work for anything. Kids grow up expecting to just be content, and then they don't know how to face problems down the road.

As I chatted with Steve, I couldn't help remembering something Focus on the Family's Dr. James Dobson said during his radio interview with me. He reflected that he could see himself being sucked right into video games if they had been available when he was in college. Imagine what this world might have missed had he become addicted to video games!

The good news for Steve is that he has turned a corner. And despite an occasional relapse, he has pretty much broken free of his addiction, enabling him to pursue more exciting opportunities.

Steve: I'm going to Europe in September. August I might be in Costa Rica; I'm going to a language school down there, to do volunteer work. It really worries me that men with great potential are never going to realize it. Up until middle school my grades were great. Once I started playing video games, my grades definitely started to drop.

> I feel like I'm trying to make up for eight years of lost potential.

That's what I've seen in the last two years. I feel like I'm trying to make up for eight years of lost potential. I'm astounded at what I can accomplish now when I devote all that time and energy to something worthwhile.

Steve's experience touches upon what I consider one of the great tragedies associated with video game addiction: the lost potential of an emerging generation. Especially, as our next chapter reveals, among young men.

6

LOST BOYS

D O YOU REMEMBER the Lost Boys of Never-Never Land? Under the leadership of Peter Pan, they refused to grow up, hoping to remain forever children at play in a world of make-believe adventures. Well, they are still around. They've simply changed locations.

Tom Chiarella is a divorced father of two boys. They play Xbox games like *Halo* in a room that resembles many bachelor pads—game console usurping the television as the centerpiece of the furniture arrangement and social connection. They often invite friends over to join in the fun. It's an increasingly common sight. There are similar rooms all over the country, with boxes, tied controllers and phone lines, televisions positioned at various angles, window shades drawn. This is the preferred province of men and boys left to their own devices—in dorm rooms, game rooms, television rooms, and dens.

"We once agreed on an hour a day, maximum," Tom re-flected in a 2004 article titled "The Lost Boys." "But it's not out of the question for us to play four or seven hours, to order pizza, to sit there and bet pennies on the number of kills we get. And I know, in some fashion, I am doing wrong by them, indulging them, letting them stay at this, deep in this dumb game. Someone ought to get them outside, get them talking about something else. But I always figure at least we're in there together, into something, learning some-thing. And there are no drugs nearby."[1]

Tom rarely wins, unable to compete with his wired-generation kids. The boys become bored with his lame efforts. Still, it gives them harmless, good-natured guy time together. Or so Tom assumed until he took his boys on a field trip to visit the boys' heroes—a tribe of gamers calling themselves the Order of Light and their leader, Suicide Bob.

Gus, Tom's fourteen-year-old boy, saw the Order of Light featured on MTV—a house full of young men with part-time jobs who lived together and spent all of their time play-ing video games. Rather than going by their given names, each was called by his high-score screen name and flaunted an identity founded entirely in their pretend realm of battles, conquests, and perilous pursuits. Gus and his buddies were very impressed by the game prowess and lifestyle of Suicide Bob and his cronies, comparing their greatness to the presi-dent of the United States or home run champ Sammy Sosa. Intrigued, Tom decided to drive his boys to Memphis to ob-serve the Order of Light in their natural habitat.

"When I told my friends that I was taking the boys to meet the Order of Light, they seemed puzzled or alarmed," Tom wrote. "Most assumed video games to be pointless, anti-social, and even bad for the economy. They saw our quest as pointless, too. 'I'm taking them to see their heroes,' I said to one friend. 'Guys playing video games?' she said. 'Some heroes.'"[2]

"Guys playing video games? Some heroes."

But they went anyway and met a group of guys who, despite their celebrity status as masters of the digital universe, looked much like the kids who drive beat-up pizza delivery trucks in every neighborhood. Their shade-drawn apartment contained everything a boy could want. In "The Lost Boys," Tom described the scene as he and his boys were invited into the inner sanctum.

The whole place is rigged and networked with the kind of inventory a thirteen-year-old dreams of—eight televisions, four personal computers, one TiVo, three Xboxes, two GameCubes, two Dreamcasts, two PlayStations, two PlayStation 2's, one PlayStation 2 equipped for Japanese games, two Neo-Geos, one Nee-Gee Pocket, two Wonder-Swans, one TurboExpress, a Game Boy Pocket, a Game Boy Calm, a Game Boy Advanced, a Game Boy Advanced SP, twenty-eight controllers, and 762 video games. Probably six hundred feet of cable ran across the floors of all four rooms. Every surface of every piece of furniture, save the couch and recliner, is covered in wires, game boxes, and hardware. In the kitchen, the only recognizable utensils are a box of fast-food straws and a glass of plastic forks. The fridge is full of Cokes.

Within minutes, we start gaming . . . Soon we've been here for four hours. Maybe longer. The shades are drawn. It might be noon, or it might be suppertime. You can never tell. Four of them sit on the couch in semidarkness, eyes turned toward the television, one of them playing a combat video game called *Soul Calibur II*. The other three watch. My children are seated at their feet. The men—and they are men (twenty-six, thirty-one, twenty-seven, twenty-five years old)—sit in various stages of dress, in poses that reflect a kind of mutual indifference to conversation. One reclines, fusses with his shoes, one flips through a gaming magazine, the other plays. All the while, they do nothing but talk, but not to one another really. It's more like a running commentary . . .

There are no signs of toothbrushes or soap in the bathroom. Nothing is made or managed or much cared for, save the games, which are held with the reverence of communion wafers.[3]

Tom asks each member of the tribe a few questions. It seems none of them gave a second thought to the possibility that they are wasting time, wasting their lives. Each wants more. Each has plans. But none were actually doing much to pursue them.

One says he is saving to move to the West Coast in, he hopes, about twelve months. Another has enrolled in flying lessons that should take four years. The third is only six elective hours shy of his university mathematics degree. He can't seem to pass one particular class. When pushed, he embarrassingly admits that it is a dumb class called Men and Women. I have no idea of the precise subject matter, but his lifestyle hardly lends itself to discovering the reality of either.

The last admits he is not really good at anything, so takes pride in his status as the tribe member who "doesn't blink," the guy who is not afraid of anything. "Not zombies, not mutant dogs. Fearless."

By the time my husband, Kurt, reached his late twenties he was a married father of two with a thriving career. These guys, by contrast, work part-time jobs and share an apartment with other gamers with no ambition to achieve more. Suicide Bob had even turned down numerous promotion opportunities at FedEx, where he has a part-time schedule, to avoid interfering with his true priorities back in his adolescent fantasy world apartment. He tried college, but only lasted six weeks, quitting to pursue working in an arcade. SB eventually found that everything he wanted could be obtained by reaching the next game level, not by working longer hours or completing his college degree. Besides, the FedEx job includes a cool benefit—one trip per year on a FedEx plane to any location on earth he'd like, which he always used to fly to a video game convention in Vegas.

Part of the problem, it seems, is the source of these boys' sense of belonging and identity. The world of video games creates a false sense of manhood by allowing them to "be successful" without demanding any of the risk or discipline required to achieve real manhood quests like career, marriage, and fatherhood. They have chosen, albeit unconsciously, the road of immediate gratification in a virtual world over long-term success and meaning offered by real-life pursuits. Unable to muster enough courage to face true risk and reward, they develop pseudo-identities—and even describe their cowardly ways as "fearless." And sadly, they seem close to convincing themselves it is true.

Tom observes nothing immoral or wrong about the Order of Light—no drugs, drinking, fights, hazing, gambling, cursing, or hard feelings. They don't watch too much television or overeat. And almost all of them go to church, usually with their folks. Still, he finds himself troubled by their zombielike existence and the trajectory of their lives.

I keep telling myself that nine men together are better than nine men on their own. I want to believe that. I know they aren't hurting anyone. And it's impossible not to like the thought of living a life like this, as cozy and snug as a children's book. These guys don't ask much. Their comforts are small, attainable, taxing no one. It's a remarkable kind of freedom really, so vaguely righteous, so oddly libertarian, that it's almost completely American. But I can't for the life of me tell what they want.

I do know what I want. I want to grab them by the shoulders and shake them. Then I want to get my kids out of there. We left the next day, the boys and I.[4]

On the way home from their hero visit, Tom realized the experience had had an impact on his boys, especially on the younger, Walter.

"I'll tell you what bothers me," Walter said. "The ambition thing. I mean, they can fly anywhere they want in the whole world, right?" referring to Suicide Bob's FedEx travel benefit. "And they don't go anywhere. I'd go to Malaysia at least, or Hawaii."[5]

Then Gus looked up at his dad and said the visit helped him figure out that he wanted to play football.

It appears Suicide Bob and his fellow tribesmen will be coming off the hero list in at least one family.

University Playland

Some might expect young men who have limited skills or opportunities to spend an excessive amount of time playing games as a means of replacing a thrill-less existence. But a growing percentage of society's best and brightest, those who should see the world as their oyster, are sacrificing their real-life potential in order to beat the next level of a game.

John Messerly, lecturer at the Department of Computer Sciences at the University of Texas at Austin, provides a snapshot of the problem.

He conducted interviews with more than a thousand students about their gaming habits in order to confirm his suspicion that game addiction was diminishing the potential of otherwise gifted young people, particularly among computer science majors. Messerly's conclusions should cause concern for any parent doling out thousands of dollars for tuition, books, room, and board in order to give their kids the opportunities afforded by a college education.

Knowing students might "sugarcoat" the reality of video game addiction, Messerly decided to ask whether they "know someone" whose social or scholastic life had been negatively affected by these games. More than 90 percent said that they did, describing "friends" who remained chained to their dorm room or apartment for days, weeks, even semesters.

Role-playing games like *EverQuest* emerge as particularly problematic among those questioned. The big allure, they admit, is escapism. "One can live in these virtual worlds," explains Messerly, "with little or no interaction with the ordinary world right now." Many students admitted that real life offers less interesting options than the exciting universes found in their games. In fact, when confronted with the possibility that Mom and Dad might not want to fund their student "wasting" time on games instead of studies, some say it is even possible to derive a living from role-playing computer games.

"Evidently," Messerly explains, "gamers create and develop characters—a time-consuming process—and sell them for profit."

I met with one such student who seemed especially pleased with his own entrepreneurial initiative for selling one such character, listing it as justification for the hundreds of hours invested. When I asked how much he had earned while wasting his parents' tuition money, he sheepishly acknowledged it was less than a hundred dollars. He laughed at himself when I pointed out that earning a few pennies per hour is hardly a promising career! But as Messerly reveals, the tendency of students to justify their time on such games continues, especially among those pursuing computer science degrees.

"As for the claim that some gaming is needed for computer science education," affirms Messerly, "I simply reject it." It's an important observation from someone who teaches computer science at the university level.

Messerly compares video games to cigarette addiction, saying those who smoke feel a need for and perceive benefits from their habit. After all, if you take away the cigarettes, they feel even greater stress due to withdrawal. His conclusion?

"Similarly, role-playing games may appear good to those playing—because they want to escape the world or are afraid of it—but for the moment the real world holds much more for those who have the courage to face it. It holds more depth, more possible experience, more knowledge, more joy, more beauty, and more love than the world of a computer-generated reality. It is possible to imagine that in the future this may no longer be the case; but for the present such escapism is cowardly."[6]

Why Boys?

In the conclusion of his report, Messerly observes that the problem of video game addiction appears most serious among young men. He notes that these games target "primal areas of the brain" and satisfy "primitive needs in the (primarily male) psyche."[7] This observation is consistent with every other study I've encountered that suggests boys and men are far more likely to become hooked than girls. As we learned in an earlier chapter, many of the games are intentionally designed with elements that play to the basic drives of the male psyche, including adventure, competition, and desire for mastery.

The teachings of my Christian faith compel men to follow the model of Jesus Christ, who said that we must lose our life to find it, and that the greatest love is to lay one's life down for another. In other words, we discover true meaning in life through self-sacrifice, not self-gratification. For men, that means finding fulfillment through the sacrificial love of marriage and fatherhood and/or building something that can contribute to the good of others. By disciplining their strengths and skills and investing in the lives of others, men play their God-ordained role in the world.

The contrast to young men investing their lives in video games couldn't be starker or sadder, because it meets those basic drives of manhood in an artificial manner that is self-focused rather than others-focused. The empty pursuit of game points, levels, adventure, sex, conquest, and domination ends up replacing meaningful goals by draining all desire for the life-renewing, God-given passions of real life.

A very different idea of manhood has emerged over the past two decades due to the video game culture. As Tom Chiarella commented after meeting Suicide Bob, "There's a subset of manhood in America: adult males who are forgoing ambition, sex, money, love, adventure to sit in darkened rooms mastering video games."[8]

Boys are preprogrammed to find fulfillment as men who build something that will improve society. Video game addiction is causing men to remain boys, building nothing more than a high score. They show little evidence of industry, self-discipline, or desire to make their world a better place.

I, for one, refuse to allow my boys to slide down that slippery slope into a cycle of emptiness they may not even realize has overtaken true joy. They, like others, could have found themselves adults unable to enjoy real life—failing to connect the dots back to video games as the source of their problem.

What parent dreams of a son growing up to become a video game hero? Little girls dream of the chance to marry a handsome prince who might win her and provide for a family—not a trigger-happy gamer who might beat the next level and invest every available dollar and moment gaming. A friend of mine shared that her daughter came home from college recently and expressed how pervasive video gaming is among college young men. "It's disgusting, Mom!" her daughter exclaimed. "The guys act like little boys. They don't socialize. They have no interest in dating. They just go to class and rush through homework in order to get back to their video games!"

As we'll see in the next chapter, even the guys who do date and marry can carry this "disgusting" pattern with them into the honeymoon.

7

TILL GAMES DO US PART
(TRUE CONFESSIONS)

BECAUSE THE VIDEO game culture has emerged over the past two decades, we are witnessing the first generation of young adults encountering the effects of game addiction in their relationships. I sat down for coffee with newlyweds Jeff and Laura. They gave me a taste of how the growing trend toward game obsession among boys carries into manhood and can, unfortunately, invade wedded bliss. Married less than a year, Laura quickly learned that games can top the list of marital conflict concerns. I asked Jeff to describe his early gaming habits.

Jeff: I started back when we were living in Houston before I was ten. But there wasn't a lot of playing, because I grew up in a home with three boys who were mostly out running around. Both my grandparents had lots of acreage, so we'd play out there. Then when we moved up here to Colorado, we started playing more computer games—on the PC until we got Nintendo 64. After that, my dad started getting into it. He would pull out his laptop and download games. It became a normal evening for him to sit down and play video games until dinner. Then we'd all eat together, and he'd go back to his chair to play. He was pretty distant for a while.

We also had a friend across the street who was a good friend of the family. We started getting together to play board games, and that turned into playing computer games. When we came home, we'd find Dad still playing.

We kept getting more advanced systems. There became a point in about late middle school or early high school where I would come home from school, start playing a game, and play until I had to do my homework and go to bed.

"Toward the end of high school and after graduation we would stay up all night until five o'clock in the morning and still be playing video and online games."

Then I would get up, go to school, come home, and do it again. All three of us played together, nights on end. Toward the end of high school and after graduation we would stay up all night until five o'clock in the morning and still be playing video and online games.

As Jeff described how much time he and his brothers spent playing games, I wondered if they were able to keep up on schooling. With Dad and the three boys playing so much and creating a mini-culture of gaming, it must have affected their grades, I guessed.

Jeff: That is definitely evident with my two brothers who are still in college. One of them has flunked out two semesters in a row due to staying up all night playing video games. The other goes to school all day, referees on weekends, and plays games all night. Most of the time he doesn't even go to school 'cause he plays video games all day and won't get off of them to go to class. He's paying for school with student loans, but he's figured out that he's running out of money, so he's got to get it done quickly. He knows he's addicted.

I think all of the men in my family have something of an addictive personality. I think that we watched our dad and we all emulated that, big-time. He'd play from six until ten, and we'd play from ten until two. He considered that okay.

It seemed easier for Jeff to see the problem in his brothers than in himself. But his wife, Laura, jumped in to give her perspective.

Laura: Jeff was just as addicted as his brothers at one point. He would play all night, without fail. He wouldn't go to classes sometimes because he had played all night. His grades started to go down in high school, from straight As his sophomore year, junior year As and Bs, and senior year to As, Bs, and Cs. I know this bothered Jeff's mom, but she didn't push the issue. She just said, "Do your own thing." Jeff's mom said to me one time, "I just gave up." I don't think she really tried that hard because she was fighting Dad and the boys, and it was really difficult.

Laura and Jeff started dating during this period of his life. I asked Laura if she saw gaming as a problem for them then and whether they had discussed it before marriage.

Laura: When we first started dating casually, I was still in high school. I had to go to sleep because I had school the next day. We both worked at a restaurant, so we were up late. But a lot of times after we had hung out until two in the morning, he'd go home and play games all night long. I would sleep in and never know because we were in different places.

On several occasions when I used to drive over to his house, he couldn't even drag himself out of bed. He would still be asleep when I got there because he had stayed up all night long and had only gotten to bed half an hour before I got there. This really started to frustrate me. We had probably been dating three or four months at the time.

There would be nights that he'd say, "Call me as soon as you get off work and I'll head over to your place." I'd call him, and two hours later he'd knock on my door, and I'd say, "What took you so long?" and he'd say, "Oh, I was playing my game." He just couldn't get off the game! I got so fed up with it!

I've noticed that slowly there are more and more girls

getting involved in it. I think because they want to hang out with the guys, and that's what the guys are doing. Really early in our relationship he was playing *Counter Strike* all the time, and at first he wanted me to sit by him and play. I told him no. One time he looked at me and said, "Well, Austin"—his ex-girlfriend—"would play *Counter Strike* with me." I said, "Then go date Austin!"

One night it was so bad we fought about it, and I was still mad when I went to work. He played the game the whole time I was at work. When I got off work, he called and said he was coming over, and I asked, "Are you coming now or later?" and he said, "I'm coming right now." I waited about an hour, thinking, "This is ridiculous!" I had pretty much made my decision. We had only been together about four months, and I thought, "I don't want to deal with this. I am not crazy enough about this guy to deal with this. I'm not going to put myself in a position where a video game is more important than I am."

So I basically told him, "We need to take a break, you need to go think about it, because I'm not going to play number two to a video game." He left, and I called my friend and cried all night. I thought it was over. But he went and talked to one of his friends too and called me back later that night and said, "You know, you're right. You shouldn't be second to a video game."

Jeff: I remember sitting in a car talking to a friend about this. He just looked at me and says, "What are you thinking? You're going to throw away the best thing in your life for a video game?" And it just snapped in my head, "Oh my gosh, what am I thinking? This is ridiculous!" I would say that was the turning point.

Laura and Jeff have been married for one year. Has the problem gone away?

Laura: We're getting there, but it's definitely still a battle. I understand it's something he wants to do. It's like a drug, he enjoys it. I could never really understand why he wants to play this game when I'm sitting right here and we could go see a movie or do something fun together.

> "I really didn't think we were going to make it, because I just couldn't take it. I did not want to be second to a video game."

I definitely don't want our kids to play at all. I don't want my son growing up and doing that. I told [Jeff's] parents, "You've made this really hard. I wish you had said, 'No games,' to Jeff, because now he has this addiction that is so hard to break." It's not like he really wants to hurt me, it's just like he can't break away from it. I really didn't think we were going to make it, because I just couldn't take it. I did not want to be second to a video game.

Jeff: I started thinking, "Oh my gosh! This is not the lifestyle I want for my children." I mentioned earlier the friend of our family who played video games with us. He used to borrow some of our games, take them home, and then his wife would drop them back off a week later. He would not stop playing them once they got in the home, so she took them and dropped them off at our house without him being aware of it.

They have two kids, and he still can't handle it now. If it's in front of him, he will play it. His wife has to hide the games throughout the house where he can't find them so that he won't play while everyone else is in bed.

Laura: Jeff told me a story about a guy he knows. Every Sunday is his gaming day. He has a wife and children, and he was complaining about his sex life. I looked at Jeff and said, "I wonder if this man took this Sunday and said, 'Honey, what would you like to do today? Let's take the day and do something with the kids.' I bet his sex life would improve 100 percent!"

Women do manage to go with the flow even when they feel so left out and neglected. Even though I know that's not what anyone intends, but that was truly how I felt for a long time. Until we got married I didn't know how often Jeff played games because I wasn't there all the time. It was a real battle for us for a while. I couldn't understand it, and it hurt my feelings. I don't think that's the mind-set of anyone playing; it's just addictive.

I think the other thing that really made a change in Jeff was when we got married and he recognized his responsibilities. At that point he started looking at some of his friends. They'd call at one in the morning, and he'd say, "What are you doing? I've got to go to work in the morning. I need sleep, don't call me." Now he looks at his brothers and says, "That's not a good lifestyle." But he was right there in it. I think it's just about taking a step out of it.

Jeff: Since we have been married, I've noticed whenever I start playing, I tend to fall more into doing it. The computer at my parents' house has all my old games on it. One time Laura went out with her girl-friends, and my parents were out of town, so I went over there and played all night. My brother was in town, so we played together until the early morning hours. I went back home, and the next night I really wanted to play again, so I said to Laura, "Do you want to go hang out with your sister?" She did. So I went to play games. Whenever I start getting back in that mind-set, I see the problem more clearly. Sitting back right now, I think I could go home and play for an hour and I'd be fine. But the truth is, if I get started playing, I seldom play for just one hour. I tell myself, "I can go to work on six hours of sleep, or five, or four."

> "I seldom play for just one hour. I tell myself, 'I can go to work on six hours of sleep, or five, or four.'"

Laura: I never want my kids to come home, all excited to see Dad, and then have him sit on the couch playing games. They'll think they're not important enough, because you're not getting off the couch to greet them. I never want my kids to think, "Dad's not available," or "I can't wait to play football with Dad! But wait, it's Sunday—his video game day." I never want my kids to feel that let down, nor do I want to feel let down. I think we need our men to be in the real world and to address real issues.

As I sat listening to Jeff and Laura, I found myself reflecting on the first few years of my marriage. I was student teaching during the day and working at night. Kurt was working full-time and getting his master's degree in the evening. The small amount of extra time that was available went to enjoying each other, taking care of household responsibilities, or doing some other activity together. I cannot imagine trying to fit hours and hours of gaming into that stage of our life.

Laura said our men should be investing themselves in the real world, dealing with real issues. They need to become real heroes to their wives and children, not imaginary heroes in an artificial realm. I worry about the millions of potentially productive, responsible young men who get so caught up "making a difference" in the virtual world that they are putting off making a life in the real one.

8

TOXIC FUN

IN JUNE 2005 *WorldNetDaily*, a daily online news source, reported that a twelve-year-old schoolboy named Sergei died as a result of his twelve-hour-per-day computer game obsession.[1] The incident occurred in a western town in Russia, where the boy's parents reportedly allowed Sergei to attend computer club as a reward for getting good grades in school.

"When this boy came last time, he felt quite good and played for almost twelve hours," an employee at the club told a newspaper reporter. "Then suddenly he fell on the floor and convulsed."

Sergei had trouble breathing and was put on a ventilator. The diagnosis was that Sergei had suffered an epileptic seizure, apparently triggered by prolonged hypertension common when playing computer and video games. Eight days after the collapse, the boy died in the hospital from a stroke.

"He was dying but could not tear himself from the game," said senior doctor Alexei Sulimov. "Brain hemor-

"He was dying but could not tear himself from the game."

rhage took place due to sustained emotional stimulation of the brain . . . This was the result of emotional stress because he was obsessed with the games. Apart from his obsession with computer games he was a healthy kid and there was no reason why he should not have had a long and healthy life."

Less than two months later a twenty-eight-year-old man in South Korea, one of the most wired countries in the world, played computer games for fifty hours almost non-stop and died of heart failure minutes after completing his mammoth session in an Internet café.[2]

Such reports, while exceptional, raise important questions about what we are allowing children and young people to do to themselves.

We've already seen how video games can drain the life out of those who become obsessed. But I am also concerned about the serious physical risks associated with video game addiction, including sudden death. The story of Shawn Woolley reveals what happens when both threats converge upon a single person.

"He shot himself because of the game"

Shawn seemed a happy kid growing up in Wisconsin despite struggling with emotional problems tied to learning disabilities. But he made it through the challenges of childhood, thanks to lots of hard work and the loving support of his mom, Liz. By twenty-one years old Shawn seemed ready to fly with his steady job and a nice apartment.

On Thanksgiving Day, 2001, Liz found Shawn's dead body in that apartment. He had shot himself while sitting at his computer in front of *EverQuest*, the online game that had become his life obsession. *EverQuest* is one of the many games known in the industry as MMORPGs (Massively Multiplayer Online Role-Playing Games). She ascertained that he had shot himself because something terrible had happened to a character he called "iluvyou"—perhaps a rejection or betrayal. "He shot himself because of the game," she told reporters.

Sony Online Entertainment president John Smedley, one of the creators of *EverQuest*, denies the game caused Woolley's death. "When I spoke with Ms. Woolley I expressed my condolences. And it's really one of those terrible things that happens. And there's just nothing to suggest that *EverQuest* had any role in his death," he says. "*EverQuest* is a game. And I don't see any connection between a form of entertainment and somebody's tragic suicide." Smedley says calling his game "addictive" is nonsense.

Shawn's grieving mother, on the other hand, thinks the game is dangerous and designed to be addictive: "I think the way the game is written is that when you first start playing it, it is fun, and you make great accomplishments. And then the further you get into it, the higher level you get, the longer you have to stay on it to move onward, and then it isn't fun anymore. But by then you're addicted, and you can't leave it."

After becoming hooked on *EverQuest,* Shawn stopped working and stopped seeing his family. "I think that was the beginning of the end," says Liz.

Since Shawn's death Liz has connected with hundreds of other people who testify that *EverQuest* addictions are ruining their lives. There is even a Web site called Everquest Widows, developed for people who suspect their loved ones and spouses have become addicted to the game.

"If somebody shoots themselves in front of a computer screen of this game," says Shawn's mom, "they're trying to say something. You don't go sit in front of a computer game and shoot yourself if it didn't have something to do with the game."[3]

Runescape, EverQuest, and *World of Warcraft* are part of a new and growing generation of computer, video, and Internet attractions drawing our children into a virtual world that is potentially toxic. To use a fitting comparison, if PlayStation and Game Boy games represent the marijuana of game addiction, Internet-based games like *EverQuest* are the equivalent of crack cocaine. Of course, not all players become hooked, and few will go as far as Shawn. But then, not everyone who plays in the street gets hit by a car. So what's the infatuation? For one thing, online games are designed to be addictive. Thirty-something Aaron Hazell of Toronto admits that he once played *Ultima*

Online for about eighteen hours per day, even skipping an occasional day at work to keep going. Why? Because the games have what he describes as "an incredible amount of depth. The possibilities are endless."

The never-ending process of expanding complexity is another draw. While the game is easy at the start, players become caught up in the cycle of moving rapidly through levels. And the longer they play, the more difficult it becomes, compelling many players to remain online no matter how long it takes.

Making matters worse, online games continue even after a player has turned off the computer, because players on the other side of the globe are just getting up to begin playing when you lie down to sleep, making you reluctant to leave the screen. "You don't want to sign out because you might miss something," says Hazell. "That's the hook."[4]

> If PlayStation and Game Boy games represent the marijuana of game addiction, Internet-based games like *EverQuest* are the equivalent of crack cocaine.

But the most potent "hook" is the chemical reaction that takes place in the player's brain. As we learned in chapter 2, a flood of dopamine generates a physiological high similar to other addictive behavioral patterns and drugs like cocaine and heroin.

From the Horses' Mouths

Writer and researcher Nicholas Yee provides one of the best analyses of this problem I've encountered, in a report titled "Ariadne—Understanding MMORPG Addiction."[5] Defining addiction as "a recurring behavior that is unhealthy or self-destructive which the individual has difficulty ending," Yee asked over two thousand *EverQuest* players whether they considered themselves addicted to the game. Nearly three-quarters indicated they might be addicted, probably were addicted, or definitely were addicted—with an amazing 35 percent saying definitely!

What types of "unhealthy or self-destructive" behavior did this group encounter? Consider responses to a series of statements posed by Yee. While female trends lagged only slightly behind those of males, I have highlighted responses from males.

1. I have played continuously for ten hours or more.
   * Aged twelve to seventeen: 60.9 percent
   * Aged eighteen to twenty-two: 66.2 percent
   * Aged twenty-three to twenty-eight: 69.7 percent
   * Aged twenty-nine to thirty-five: 63.5 percent
   * Over thirty-five: 58.6 percent
2. I often lose sleep because of my playing habits.
   * Aged twelve to seventeen: 46.6 percent
   * Aged eighteen to twenty-two: 50.7 percent
   * Aged twenty-three to twenty-eight: 41.1 percent

- Aged twenty-nine to thirty-five: 40 percent
- Over thirty-five: 45.2 percent

3. I would consider myself addicted to the game.
  - Aged twelve to seventeen: 66.7 percent
  - Aged eighteen to twenty-two: 62.2 percent
  - Aged twenty-three to twenty-eight: 45.2 percent
  - Aged twenty-nine to thirty-five: 42.3 percent
  - Over thirty-five: 48.3 percent

4. I have tried to quit the game but was unsuccessful.
  - Aged twelve to seventeen: 30 percent
  - Aged eighteen to twenty-two: 20.6 percent
  - Aged twenty-three to twenty-eight: 11.8 percent
  - Aged twenty-nine to thirty-five: 10.4 percent
  - Over thirty-five: 6.4 percent

Reasons for the progressive decline on question 4 are unclear. Possibilities include fewer trying to quit as they age, or more reasons or motivation to quit as one ages, or simply the fact that it is much more difficult to stop when younger. An incredibly high 66 percent of teen players admit to addiction, almost 20 percentage points higher than adult *EverQuest* gamers.

Those polled also provided insight into their emotional reactions to the game. Respondents include many who play on a casual basis, not just those indicating addiction.

1. I become anxious, irritable, or angry if I am unable to play.
  - Strongly agree or agree: 15.5 percent

- Neutral: 18.4 percent
- Disagree or strongly disagree: 65.6 percent

2. I continue to play even when I am upset or frustrated with the game and not really enjoying it.
   - Strongly agree or agree: 28.8 percent
   - Neutral: 21.2 percent
   - Disagree or strongly disagree: 49.5 percent

3. My playing habits have caused me academic, health, financial, or relationship problems.
   - Strongly agree or agree: 18.4 percent
   - Neutral: 13.2 percent
   - Disagree or strongly disagree: 68 percent

The more dramatic story here lies below the surface of the combined statistics. Those who play an average of between four and six hours per day indicated much higher rates of anxiety, anger, and the other negative outcomes tracked in the survey. In fact, over 50 percent of those who average four hours per day of playtime indicated they continue playing even when they are not enjoying the game, and recognize that their habits have created academic, health, financial, or relationship problems!

So why do they do it? Like other

> Over 50 percent of those who average four hours per day of playtime indicated they continue playing even when they are not enjoying the game, and recognize that their habits have created academic, health, financial, or relationship problems!

addictions, it may start with fun and games—even generating an increased sense of well-being. But over time, that degenerates into lower self-esteem and self-respect. Less than 25 percent of respondents said they feel better about themselves when playing.

Statistics are helpful, but fail to tell the whole tale. Below are samples of how *EverQuest* addicts feel about the problem, in their own words as quoted in Yee's report.

> I play EQ for 18 month now. And when I take all time of my characters and calculet the average I played 4h a day. This is mad. I tryed to stop playing EQ for some month, because I had to do a excam. But I found me everyday looking through the internet and reading EQ sites. I often find me thinking about EQ and daydreaming. I am addicted and know that, and I like it. [Male, aged twenty-four]

> I do think i am an EQ addict, and yes I have tryd to stop. This was after i got my brother hookd on it tho, so even after i quit, he beggd me to get back on to play with him. I held out for a long time, but I eventualy crackd, and got re-addicted. I think i like EQ, but i cant be shure. Its just to damn addicting to know if i actuialy enjoy the game. You might say, "well you would know if you like it or not" Well that might be true for some, but i just dont know. [Male, aged seventeen]

> Yes, I consider myself addicted to EQ. I haven't tried quitting yet, but I will have to in a few months. I don't spend

enough time with my 2 1/2 year old daughter. I'm a full-time mom, and my daughter watches TV all day while I play the game. In September, I will start home schooling her, so I'll have to cut down on my EQ time. I'd like to stop now so I would have time to take her to the park during the week, or even let her play in the backyard, but leveling, getting new spells and new skills is all I think about. [Female, aged twenty-seven]

I am addicted to EQ and I hate it and myself for it. When I play I sit down and play for a minimum of 12 hours at a time, and I inevitably feel guilty about it, thinking there [are] a large number of things I should be doing instead, like reading or furthering my education or pursuing my career. But I can't seem to help myself, it draws me in every time. I have been out of work now for over a month and now find myself in a stressful, depressed state that is only quelled when I am playing EQ, because it's easy to forget about real world troubles and problems, but the problem is when you get back to the real world, problems and troubles have become bigger, and it's a bad, bad cycle. I've tried quitting seriously on several occassions, but I was shocked to find each time that the experience reminds of what I've heard quitting heroin is like. There are serious withdrawal pangs, anxiety, and a feeling of being lost and not quite knowing what next to do with yourself. I don't think this could possibly be the norm for most people, maybe I just have an addictive personality, although I've never been addicted to anything before in my life. [Male, aged twenty-six]

Many of Yee's respondents gave reasons for why they felt the game was so addictive. Oft cited was that it allowed players to escape the real world.

> I think anyone that plays more than 20 hours a week is addicted tho most would deny it. The sad truth is that in many ways EQ is better than RL. It is easier to succeed in EQ, I can be beautiful, fit and healthy in EQ—in real life I am chronicly ill and there isn't much fun or achievement to be had. EQ is more than just an opiate, and much more than just a game. In a very real sense EQ gives me an opportunity to feel free. [Female, aged thirty-six]

Other players talked about the friends and social obligation factor.

> I am an EQ addict. I play every day, only taking a break when I get to a point where I have real life stress over something that happens in game. When I do take breaks, it's usually for only a day. I worry about my game life as much as I worry about my real life. If I am late getting on, I feel like people will be disappointed with me. As a guild leader, when conflicts arise people come to me to resolve them. People look to you to have events, help them get things, quest, etc. I have had people in my own guild leave because they didn't feel we gave them enough of our time or enough "phat lewt." I try to please everyone, but it is unrealistic to think you can be everywhere for everyone, keeping them all happy. It gets to be a heavy burden to bear, and sometimes I end up in tears out of frustration. I am an addict. Will I quit? No. Why? Because I love it. [Female, aged thirty]

Still others attribute the addictive draw to the constant lure of "the next best thing."

> The game is set up to make you want the next best thing. "Oh look what that guy has! How do I get that?" The answer is always to spend more time online either getting to a higher level to go camp the item, or to just go camp the item (or slight variation, camp the quest items that result in the new item). But you are rewarded for playing more. Better items, more freedom on where you can go. [Male, aged twenty-one]

Sadly, many who do quit find themselves hooked into playing again.

> I had been playing EQ for about 2 months when I began to realize the amount of time I was spending away from reality and my obligations. I gradually weaned myself off EQ after another 2 months. I haven't played EQ regularly for a few months now. Although I have regained some control, I still feel serious urges to play now and again. EQ has a very distinct society that I found appealing. Everyone who played found something they liked a lot and just kept doing it. Repetition and social interaction is what addicted me to EQ. I would wager to say that I am still addicted even though I don't play for long stretches at a time. EQ is highly addictive and quitting entirely is something VERY difficult to do. After all, if you do quit . . . everything you worked so hard for (your stats, equipment, friends) is gone forever since characters are stored

solely on the Verant servers. The only thing you can take with you is the stories. And those anecdotes will haunt you endlessly until you give in to the urge to re-immerse yourself in Norrath just one more time. [Male, aged twenty-seven]

Clearly, the story of games like *EverQuest* is one of isolation, compulsion, even death—if not by physical suicide, by the gradual withdrawal from the beauty and passion real life can offer.

9

DARK ISOLATION

(TRUE CONFESSIONS)

I N J U N E 2 0 0 5 eighteen-year-old Devin Moore was arrested for allegedly shooting three police officers in a copycat killing spree. His inspiration? A best-selling video game called *Grand Theft Auto,* which Devin played day and night for months before the shooting.

An attorney named Jack Thompson, a longtime crusader against video game violence, brought suit against the video game industry. His claim? That Devin Moore was, in effect, trained to do what he did because he was given a "murder simulator."

"He bought it as a minor," said Thompson. "He played it hundreds of hours, which is primarily a cop-killing game. It's our theory, which we think we can prove to a jury in Alabama, that, but for the video-game training, he would not have done what he did."[1]

Moore had no criminal history prior to June 7, 2005, when he was brought into the station on suspicion of stealing a car. It was then that he slipped into his *Grand Theft Auto* persona—shooting three police officers in the head before running into the parking lot and taking off in a police cruiser. After his capture Devin Moore reportedly told police, "Life is like a video game. Everybody's got to die sometime."[2]

Six years earlier a similar connection was illustrated in the shooting spree at Columbine High School when two boys in trench coats entered their school and opened fire on students before killing themselves. Their inspiration, according to many in the know, was a dark game called *Doom*.

Obviously, such stories represent a tiny fraction of kids who have problems far more complex than excessive time in front of a video game. Very few kids have acted out the violence they experience on-screen. Studies do show, however, that the brain sees violent video games as if the violence were real,[3] prompting concern that such "harmless fun" might not be so harmless, after all.

In 2005 the American Psychological Association urged the video game industry to curtail the violence because, among other reasons, it is bad for children's health. Research indicates that exposure to violence in video games increases aggressive thoughts, aggressive behavior, and angry feelings among youth. Studies of video games and interactive media show that the perpetrators of violence go unpunished 73 percent of the time—sending the wrong message to kids.[4]

While the focus of this book is video game addiction rather than the troubling content of games, it is important that we understand some of the feelings and experiences of kids who are drawn to the more disturbing titles. I sat down to chat with Rick, a twenty-seven-year-old who attributes much of his own descent into angry darkness to video game addiction. He told us that he could relate to the Columbine shooters—and even shared their fantasy to carry out such game simulations in real life.

Rick appears shy and withdrawn, like someone who grew up ignored or teased by childhood peers, someone who wanted to escape painful rejection. Our conversation began with Rick describing his entry into the world of video games.

Rick: I started at about age eleven playing the old Atari 2600, quickly progressing to Nintendo and other more advanced systems. I played games pretty much nonstop, and that was a big problem for me. I just would keep playing until I had to go to sleep, and sometimes even then I wouldn't stop. At the beginning the games were very simplistic. You couldn't really sit and play a game for hours on end, you would get bored, so I alternated between games. But by the time the Nintendo Entertainment System came around, there were new games coming out known as role-playing games, or RPGs. That was a big thing, what I was really into, the RPGs and adventure games where there's a story line. You play characters and advance through levels and get various skills, magic spells, and things like that.

Those games are very long; they require forty to fifty hours of playtime to finish a game. When you space that out over a few months, it's not that long. But when you're doing it constantly, it only takes a week or so to play through one. There were times I played in the middle of the night and my folks didn't know. I had a TV in my bedroom and had the system hooked up to that. Even though my room was right above theirs, I was very quiet. My parents did catch me a couple times. But they just said, "No more now, you can play tomorrow." I would wait until they went to sleep and then start playing again. By this time I was in my early teens, middle school and high school.

The majority of the time I was doing this was during summer vacations. I didn't do it too much when I was in school. When I was in school, I would play instead of doing homework, but I would generally get myself to sleep just because I had to get up early. But during the summer break I didn't have to get up early; my folks didn't force me to get up at any particular time, so I could sleep as late as I wanted.

Like many kids in his situation, Rick had very few interests apart from video games. He played an occasional game of pickup baseball with neighborhood friends in the summer, but never joined any sport leagues. He lost his interest in reading after he started playing games. Rick didn't even watch much television. On the whole, he was pretty isolated from others.

Rick: After starting video games I pretty much stopped reading except for gaming magazines, which don't really count as reading. Most of my friends weren't really into video games; the ones that were grew out of it, but I didn't. There weren't any girls I knew that wanted to play games. I was afraid of girls for a long time. I didn't want to learn about what girls were interested in because I just wanted to play games.

"After starting video games I pretty much stopped reading except for gaming magazines."

I can't say with certainty looking back that the isolation I felt at school was due to my playing video games or if I was into video games because I felt isolated. I don't know for sure what was the cause and what was the effect. But I did feel fairly isolated. I had a few friends, but no real good friends. I didn't have anybody I could really talk to.

Most of the kids that I went to school with weren't very nice to me, and I was very uptight too. I wasn't really able to laugh at myself; I never had that instilled in me as a child, that ability to not take myself so seriously. If someone said something to me and was just kidding around, I would take it as an insult; I never took it as they're just trying to make me laugh.

There were some other kids who played video games as a hobby, but there weren't many people who were as into it as I was. A lot of times when I was talking about it or writing about it, my friends wanted to be doing something else; they weren't interested in it. So I spent a lot of time by myself because that's what I was interested in, and they weren't.

I didn't spend as much time with my parents either. Before I started playing video games, I would be out in the living room with them watching TV, interested in what they were doing a good portion of the time. When I started playing video games, I was in my room all the time. I wasn't into what they were doing or even cared too much.

I don't want to blame my parents, but my dad wasn't much of an outdoor person when I was growing up. He is a math professor very into cerebral things, and he likes to play chess a lot. I enjoyed doing that with him as well, until I got into video games. Then we didn't play much anymore.

He tried playing video games with me a few times, but he wasn't really as into them as I was. He took a little bit of interest in seeing what I was playing, and there was a time, probably during his "midlife crisis," where he had a sports car, and then he liked to play racing games. I actually bought a racing wheel for one of the video game consoles I had and bought as many racing games as I could, trying to get him interested.

Beyond his relationships, Rick says his video game obsession also led to some academic struggles, including failing several classes because he played games when he should have been studying. But he describes his real problems beginning when he dived into some of the more violent games with dark themes.

Rick: I was into violent and horrific types of things. That's what I was interested in at that age, and that's kind of what was happening; I was seeking that stuff out. The more I got into it, the more I needed to satisfy whatever that craving was, and it would only be satisfied for so long before it would become a void again.

At the time, it wasn't that I didn't realize there was an issue, I just didn't really care. It's what I wanted to do and wanted to be. By the time I was about fourteen years old, I would say 75 to 80 percent of my identity was tied to the world of games. I had a fairly vivid imagination at the time, even though the majority of what I was doing in terms of video games didn't require imagination.

When I wasn't playing them, I was imagining and creating things, writing and drawing things related to those roles—another sign that they were a large part of my identity. I can remember plenty of times breaking the controller, throwing it against the wall, because I got upset with myself or the game, but I kind of grew out of that by the time I was seventeen or eighteen. I did have times that I would get very angry when things wouldn't go my way in a game, and I'd be elated when things did.

I often played games when I didn't even enjoy it. I played them because I felt like I had to complete them, especially with a lot of those role-playing games. I realized in the last two or three years I hate role-playing games, I really don't enjoy playing them. But at the time, I was doing it to complete the story. A lot of times my goal was just to complete it. I can remember hundreds of times beating games, getting to the end, and just being so disappointed in the ending and how the story was wrapped up.

There were times when I had been playing for hours on end without doing anything and my parents would get upset, telling me I needed to do something else, get outside, clean my room, something. But they never really sat down with me and said, "This is a problem we need to work on," usually because when they would yell at me and tell me I needed to do something, I'd go do it and stay away from the games for a few days—or at least make them think I was—and then go back to it.

The ultimate goal for me was always to be able to get back to the games, so sometimes I would tell my parents what I thought they wanted to hear, or do things I thought they wanted me to do to get back in their favor, and then go back to playing games as I wanted to.

There was a long period of time I didn't care about real life at all. If I could have poured myself into some sort of virtual reality setup and lived in a computer, I probably would have.

As a teen I was very unhappy, and I don't want to say it was completely and utterly because of games, but that was definitely a part of it. It made me look at my life in comparison to the lives of people in the game, and it seemed like the characters I was controlling had it so much better than I did. I didn't really have it that bad, but it made me feel worse.

When I was about eighteen, I played a lot of very violent video games. I started to become like the two kids at Columbine. There were a lot of people who made fun of me for being antisocial, and I took all of the negative emotions that I had from that and put them into doing the violent things in the video games. I imagined that the people that I was shooting in the games were these people who were causing me pain in real life.

I started out playing games for fun, and it eventually got to a point where though it was what I did, it wasn't really fun. It's just what I did. After I got out of high school, for probably the next year and a half I stayed on that path, and I was probably nineteen or twenty before I was faced with what I was becoming. I had to make a choice to either become that vile, horrible thing that I saw myself becoming, and start doing horrible things in real life, or I had to turn around. Since then I've been developing a personality. I would say that the whole time I spent gaming it certainly did have a huge effect on personality, because for a long period of time that's pretty much all I did.

> "I imagined that the people that I was shooting in the games were these people who were causing me pain in real life."

I asked Rick how he might have responded at age fourteen or fifteen if his parents had said, "We're taking this away, but we're going to start replacing it with healthy activities."

Rick: I probably would have rebelled at first. I don't think there's any question about that, I would have argued with them about it, I wouldn't have wanted that to happen. But if they stuck with it, really made it a point, I probably would have begun to see they were correct, that it was a good thing. If they were wishy-washy, I would have gone right back to it.

When I couldn't play games, I was doing something else involved with games. They didn't have portable games then, or I probably would have played them too. I read a lot of video game books and magazines at the dinner table.

If parents find that video games are all their kids want to do or talk about, that it is defining who they are and they don't have any other interests, they probably have a problem.

As I listened to Rick tell his story, my heart ached for him. I am glad that he finally broke free of his addiction. But he had lost so many years of potential joy to the isolating world of games containing very dark, violent themes that do not belong in the hands of kids. No, Rick did not go to the extreme of a school shooting or police station murder spree. Few do. He did, however, enter a similar vortex of isolation, negativity, and anger. While he may not have taken someone else's life, he did rob much of his own.

Journalist Jeff Hooten tells the story of his own deep dive into the most violent games—something he did not for fun, but to find out what kids who play such games experience. Those kids, by the way, tend to be much younger than the M rating is intended to exclude. Hooten describes the progression of killing: from a few opponents to many, from simple weapons to complex, from hesitant to quick trigger finger. He explains the physiological process overtaking his body: from increased blood pressure to accelerated pulse to rapid-fire brain neurons. He relates to the process Rick described—a drive to play driven by something other than enjoyment.

Jeff: Completing each episode elicits relief more than anything. I can stop now. I should stop now. Why am I not stopping now? I glance at the time. I'm surprised, though not really shocked, to see that I've already been at this for a couple hours. C'mon—just one more level . . . I'm tense, I'm sweating, and more than once I catch myself jitterbugging in my chair, my torso lunging and recoiling with each engagement. I'm pitted against demons and wraiths and lost souls, and to win, I must enter the video game version of hell itself . . .

Perhaps I'm playing simply because I can, because I want to know that I'm not too old, that time hasn't passed me by, that a game that any preteen can master will not get the best of me. Another half-hour goes by. I'm pathetic, I think. Go to bed.

Okay, but not until I finish this level.

I prowl subterranean passages with murderous intent. I shoot first and ask questions never, and then I shoot some more. I learn to kill subconsciously, involuntarily. I know it's just a game, but my sympathetic nervous system does not. Science tells me that exposure to violent imagery triggers in my brain a melee of limbic activity . . . In other words, I stop thinking and start reacting. Yet with repeated exposure, with each triumph or defeat, those physiological fluctuations will diminish in intensity, until my synapses record nary a flicker. Voila! Desensitization.[5]

If a grown man merely playing for research finds himself drawn into the addictive lure and desensitizing effect of such games, is it any wonder that young kids get hooked?

Rating Games

Despite the many voices of concern among psychologists, politicians, religious leaders, educators, and others, we must accept the unfortunate reality that violent, dark themes will continue to permeate video games. We must also face the fact that such games will be marketed and made available to our kids.

Thus far, the self-regulated video game rating system is the only readily available tool for parents trying to determine which games their children can or can't play. Video game ratings carry one of six logos showing age recommendations; a seventh indicates a pending rating.

 EC (Early Childhood): may be suitable for ages 3+. Contains no material that parents would find inappropriate.

 E (Everyone): may be suitable for ages 6+. May contain minimal violence, some comic mischief, and/or mild language.

 E10+ (Everyone 10+): may be suitable for ages 10+. May contain more cartoon, fantasy, or mild violence; mild language; and/or minimal suggestive themes.

 T (Teen): may be suitable for ages 13+. May contain violent content, mild or strong language, and/or suggestive themes.

M (Mature): may be suitable for ages 17+. May contain mature sexual themes, more intense violence, and/or strong language.

 AO (Adults Only): content suitable only for adults. May include graphic depictions of sex and/or violence. Adults Only products are not intended for persons under the age of 18.

 RP (Rating Pending): Titles have been submitted and are awaiting final rating.

The games also give content descriptors, listing their violence; language; tobacco, drug, and alcohol use; and sexual themes and sexual violence.

The rating system may offer some help, but it cannot be trusted. In 2004 the National Institute on Media and the Family gave the current rating system a C− on ratings education and a B− for ratings accuracy. Even more troubling, they gave the retail industry a D for enforcement. One year later the industry received lower grades in two areas, with ratings accuracy going down from a B− to a failing grade, suggesting a not-so-gradual deterioration of the entire system.

Category	2005 Grade
Ratings education (educating consumers)	C+
Ratings accuracy	F
Retailers' enforcement of policies	D−

If you are interested in a complete report please visit www.mediafamily.org. After years criticizing the Entertainment Software Rating Board (ESRB) ratings and calling for improvement of the system, the experts at the National Institute on Media and the Family say they have concluded that the system itself is beyond repair![6] Examples of the problem abound.

> The experts at the National Institute on Media and the Family have concluded that the rating system is beyond repair!

A 2004 study titled "Violence in Teen-Rated Video Games" from the Center on Media and Child Health at Boston's Children's Hospital provides specific examples of how the rating system falls short. Consider the T-rated video game *Enter the Matrix* as an example of the confusion. The R-rated films upon which these games were based, *The Matrix* and *The Matrix Reloaded*, depicted significantly *less* violence and fewer human deaths per hour than the games. But parents who might never allow their thirteen-year-old to watch the R films is comfortable renting a T game that contains far more troubling content.

Sexual content, inappropriate language, and substance abuse are also problems. The T-rated *Tony Hawk's Pro Skater 4*, for example, features the image and voice of adult film star Jenna Jameson. In behind-the-scenes film clips the porn star's character, among other sexualized antics, raises and lowers her skirt quickly, poses provocatively, and lifts her top as she exclaims, "Damn, they're bigger than I thought they were!" This same game depicts college frat boys standing on beer kegs drinking beer.

The T-rated *Tom Clancy's Splinter Cell* received no content descriptor warning for profanity, yet it contained eleven uses of inappropriate language and music from an album that required a Parental Advisory Label for Explicit Content. Such examples show why parents who have been trained to rely upon such labels in other media categories cannot assume the same accountability when it comes to video game labeling.[7]

There are billions and billions of dollars to be made, and the industry will do all it can to skirt restrictions. It is, like everything else, up to moms and dads to protect their children from the kind of experience that drove a young Rick, and many others, toward the dark brink of despair. In the next chapter, I offer suggestions on how parents should approach selecting the least addictive and harmful video games for their children.

CHAPTER

10

GIVING KIDS ANOTHER LIFE

WHEN WE LEFT off our story in chapter 1, we had
boxed up Kyle's GameCube system as a "temporary" solution to an emerging problem. I then
delved into the research you have now read on the problem of
video game addiction—and what I found convinced me I
needed to get rid of ours entirely. For our family it wasn't
worth the risks involved. No easy decision or process.

My husband and I were in complete agreement that the
video games had to go. We didn't agree, however, on the
method of disposal. Kurt wanted to sell off each item on
eBay, recouping a portion of the five hundred dollars we had
spent. The system alone had cost over one hundred dollars,
the games several hundred more—much of which came
from gift and allowance money the boys had earned. Despite
sharing Kurt's frugal inclination, I had a different, stronger

impulse. I felt we needed to throw everything in the trash on the next garbage pickup day, for several reasons.

First, fresh on the heels of a bad experience with our children and my findings about video games in general, I didn't feel right about passing the problem on to some other uninformed parent with a potentially addicted kid.

Second, I knew that I had to act quickly or risk second-guessing the decision. My children could be very convincing when it came to games. The next time they looked at me with those "Can't we play just one hour?" eyes of desperation, I feared I would cave in and soften my stance. But my kids needed me to intervene and remove the temptation. So that's what I did. Friday morning, shortly before the truck pulled up to our driveway, I gathered everything together and placed it in the waste container. Never before had the word "waste" seemed more fitting. As the truck pulled away, the knot in my stomach relaxed.

When I told Kurt what I had done, he smiled in solidarity. Now came the hard part—telling the kids.

I will never forget the look on the boys' faces when the painful reality finally sank in. Their games, their system, their "precious"—gone forever! Keep in mind, Kyle was nearly fourteen years old by this time, and video games had been a big part of his life since age seven. Shaun, at eleven, had spent five years playing. Their panicked objections came, with the most difficult tied to the money: "But we paid for those games ourselves!" Understandably, they felt a great injustice had occurred.

Kurt and I had already thought of our response and assured the kids that it was not their fault. We told them that we had decided to pay them the money they had spent, dollar for dollar, to spend on other hobbies. We felt it was important to make sure the boys knew they had done nothing wrong—so they would not be penalized. Without question, we consider that to be the best investment we've ever made. The replacement money was spent on summer camp, golf clubs, board games, vacation spending money, and all manner of "natural" fun.

Still, the coming months were challenging. As the child who had played the longest, Kyle struggled most. We were caught off guard as he experienced a season of depressive lows, something we now realize were symptoms of withdrawal from years and years of chemically induced "highs" in the brain. We now tell parents who decide to remove video games from the home to prepare themselves for a season of symptoms like agitation and depression, similar to those experienced by many smokers going cold turkey.

One evening shortly after the disappearance of his games, Kyle opened up to his dad. It had been a particularly difficult day; every one of his buddies at school had excitedly discussed the latest big-release game while Kyle sat and listened, unable to enter into what had become a primary point of social connection among the boys. Feeling cut off from his friends, thanks to overly strict parents, Kyle expressed his frustration that something he loved doing had been taken away.

"We've discussed this before, Kyle," was Kurt's sympathetic but firm reply. "It won't always be this hard. The longer you stay away from games, the easier it will become."

"I know, Dad," Kyle said with tortured emotion. "But there's no 'patch' for video games!" His severe withdrawal symptoms highlighted the need for something to ease the transition, like a nicotine patch or gum for smokers. Unfortunately, nothing of the sort exists to help game addicts through the difficult days.

> "There's no 'patch' for video games!"

It took about six months for Kyle to move through the withdrawal process. By that time he had developed a love for several alternatives, including some board and card games. We also brought into our home something we had never expected to own. Kurt had always resisted the notion of getting a pet. But we agreed (after the kids and I ganged up on Dad) that a playful dog would be just the thing to fill the void left by the digital drug dispenser. On Christmas morning our children were thrilled to see a little white puppy scurry into our lives. We named him Miracle, because it was a miracle we ever got a dog!

Avoiding Common Mistakes

After that "cold turkey" season, our home became a different place. Our boys, Kyle included, reacquired a taste for more enriching ways to fill their free time. They still played an occasional video game at the home of a friend or on a special evening out at the local family fun center. We also kept our educational computer software games, which our children find much easier to turn off after a reasonable amount of play. But the fact that video games are no longer in our home eliminates the option most of the time.

About a year after the garbage truck drove away with our games, I had a wonderful moment with my son. Reviewing the list of potential school clubs during his first week of high school, Kyle noticed a listing for the Gaming Club. He looked at me and made a comment about what a waste such a club would be. We exchanged knowing smiles.

Kurt and I are glad we made the tough decision to remove video games when we did. For our home it was the best option. But we also wish the problem had never surfaced. Unfortunately, we made all of the common mistakes that can feed video game addiction in children.

Mistake 1: Starting Young

The earlier a child begins playing electronic games, the sooner he or she is exposed to the patterns that lead to addiction. Children who become accustomed to junk food lose their appetite for healthful foods. Similarly, kids also "acquire a taste" for how they want to spend their recreational time. Those who develop patterns of "natural" play, rather than "virtual" play, are more likely to become well-rounded, happy adolescents. Those who are introduced to the dopamine-inducing high of prolonged video game play often become bored with any other form of recreation.

Mistake 2: Easy Access

The vast majority of children over eight years old own their own video game system—more than one when you include handheld systems such as Game Boy. The risk of video game addiction increases dramatically when your child owns a system, because it is much harder to control the amount of time spent in an environment where it is readily available. Making matters worse, 49 percent of kids are allowed to keep the video game system in their bedrooms, where it is all but impossible to monitor time played.[1]

As with any other behavioral addiction, easy and frequent access to the object of obsession makes it more difficult to avoid potential pitfalls. Therefore, if you fear your child might become addicted, seriously consider *not* purchasing a system. They can still play once in a while at a friend's home. If you do own a system, consider purchasing only group games or E-rated racing games, and treat the system like a board game that is kept in a box and brought out periodically for an hour or so, then boxed up and returned to the closet. Such approaches can drastically reduce the risk of obsession without totally eliminating games from a child's experience. Also try to stay away from games that are designed to be played alone for long periods of time.

Mistake 3: Using as a Reward System

Many parents admit that the promise of video game playtime is the only thing they have found that can successfully motivate their child to do homework, chores, and other productive activities. And while the benefit of completed school assignments and other tasks may seem like a positive aspect of video game obsession, the long-term negative consequences far outweigh any short-term gain. Using video games as a child's motivation for completing responsible activities subconsciously reinforces the notion that completing a job, reading, learning, etc., are necessary evils to endure rather than rewards in and of themselves. Other motivational rewards, such as money, an ice-cream date with Dad, or a movie outing, are far more effective and avoid feeding a propensity toward video game obsession.

Mistake 4: "One More Level?"

When asked to shut off the video game system, it is a rare child who obeys quickly and ceases play. Invariably, they respond instead with a plea for "just one more level" or time to defeat the current villain before they will "save my game." As a result, many parents end up allowing their child to spend much more time playing video games than they intended or often realize. As one recovering video game addict said, "If you say you intend to restrict the amount of time a child spends, you better ask yourself whether you can really do it. Kids are very good at pushing and pushing for more time." Time flies when kids play video games, in part because we parents fall into the "one more level" trap.

Mistake 5: Ignoring Your Gut

Many parents have a bad feeling about the amount of time their child spends playing, talking about, and thinking about video games. There is a nagging sense that allowing so much video game time may have long-term negative consequences. But they second-guess the feeling, writing it off as being old-fashioned or too strict, thinking, "It's just the way kids are nowadays!" Besides, they don't want the inevitable conflict that comes from restricting or removing the game system. But video game addiction affects a growing number of kids, especially boys. Parents know their child better than anyone else; I urge them to trust their gut and intervene if needed to help their child live a more fulfilling life.

Advice on Intervention

Yes, video and computer games have become a dominant medium in our culture. But like every other important matter in a child's life, moms and dads have the opportunity and obligation to make wise choices that will protect a child's health and well-being. That is why we wrote this book: to give parents the information we wish we had had before making so many mistakes.

> With a bit of forethought and intentionality, you can avoid passively going along with the crowd.

The fact is, few of today's parents have given a thought to the issue of video game addiction. As a result, they are making the same mistakes we made, and more. But with a bit of forethought and intentionality, you can avoid passively going along with the crowd.

For parents dealing with a child who seems able to handle

video games as a small part of an otherwise balanced life, the following may be helpful as you try to limit the risk of addiction by selecting the least harmful games. In short, parents can use the list of driving forces of game addiction described in chapter 4 as a guide, using the following "cheat sheet."

Addictive Game Elements

Each of these elements increases the addictive draw of video games. Use the guide that follows to select the least harmful games.

Addictive Element	Key Question	Yes/No
Beat the Game	Do I compete against the system and/or myself, encouraging isolation?	———
Competition	Do I compete against other players, creating more/ longer game scenarios?	———
Mastery	Does the game include progressively more challenging levels of mastery?	———
Exploration	Must I go to hidden or secret locations to discover clues, rewards, etc.?	———
High Score	Must I achieve a certain score to enjoy the game?	———
Role Playing	Am I playing the part of a character in a story/ adventure?	———

| Relationships | Does the game allow me to build relationships with other unknown players via the Internet? | _____ |

- Game includes one or two elements: Low Risk
- Game includes three or four elements: Modest Risk
- Game includes five or more elements: High Risk

Certain genres tend to contain more of these elements than others. I've observed that online role playing and MMORPGs (see chapter 8) are by far the most addictive. Among off-line games, shy away from the role-playing adventure category. Instead, look for group party games like *Dance Revolution, Congo Bongo,* and *Mario Party,* which contain only a few addictive elements.

Keep in mind that any game can feed obsession in a child prone to get hooked. But for those dealing with children not yet obsessed, I suggest asking the salesperson about the particular elements a given game contains before renting or buying for your child.

I have intentionally avoided including an evaluation of game content. For specific content reviews I suggest you visit one of the many Web sites trying to provide such information, including www.mediafamily.org and www.pluggedinonline.org. Unfortunately, reviewing the content of a fifty-hour game requires a great deal of effort; I have not found anyone who offers comprehensive reviews. So the only safe strategy is to sit with your child while he or she is playing the game to make sure content at every level is appropriate.

For parents concerned that their child may lean toward video game obsession, I offer the following advice for different ages and stages.

Young Children (Under Ten Years Old)

As I mentioned earlier, one of the biggest mistakes parents can make is allowing their child to start playing video games too early. Remember, children will develop a taste for whatever entertainment options they are allowed to play. The earlier children begin playing video games, the more likely it is they will end up playing at dependent levels. Outside activities, sports, bike riding, reading, board games, imaginative pretending, building cardboard forts, and the many other activities that should be part of healthy childhood play cannot compete with the kind of stimulation video games afford to a child's developing brain. Our kids, for example, engaged in all of the activities listed above. But over time they became less interested in such things due to the draw of readily available video games.

Fortunately, parents of a young child (under seven) are in a wonderful position when it comes to preventing video game addiction. I recommend that they simply avoid the problem entirely by not owning a system. Digital games and their systems are very expensive, draining from the budget money better spent on fun, active, and educational toys. Never allow the child to develop a preference for video games, and you will thank yourself when they are older. If you don't, I'll return your money in full!

The middle elementary years (ages seven to ten) are probably the most important season of a child's life for parents to become intentional about video games. In most cases the child already owns a system and/or handheld device. Conscientious parents rarely allow their child to buy extremely violent games—assuming such intervention is enough to keep him or her from becoming a problem. But Mom or Dad may have begun noticing periodic agitation, disinterest in positive activities, isolation, or other behavioral and attitudinal patterns that cause concern. Perhaps the child consistently spends or wants more game time than he or she should, suggesting the beginnings of an addictive pattern.

In such cases I strongly encourage parents to box up the game systems for a prolonged season to break the pattern. After several months, if the child has developed a taste for healthy activities, you may consider bringing the games out for occasional use with very specific time limits. Another option would be to keep only the party games such as *Dance Revolution,* or some racing games that require multiple players and create a time-limited, interactive experience rather than screen-staring, solitary zombies.

If, on the other hand, your child falls right back into the same pattern of addiction, consider getting rid of the games entirely. Take time to explain to your children your concerns, share some of the research on addiction, and remind them that as in many other areas of their lives, you are doing this because you love them and want the best for them. At this age children are old enough to make you feel bad about the decision, protest the "injustice," and pressure you to change your mind. But they are also young enough to fall in line once you've made it clear the decision is final, especially if you take the time to replace it with activities that include time spent with you.

Early Adolescence (Eleven to Fourteen)

We wish we had understood the addictive nature of games before our oldest son reached age fourteen. It would have been much easier to intervene had he not spent seven years developing a compulsive love for his box and handheld. But, like many reading this book, we had to play the cards we were dealt. Usually, that means learning about the cliff of game addiction after a child is racing toward the edge. Looking back on how we handled our son's situation, I offer a few suggestions to minimize the risk of serious conflict and/or rebellion.

First, if you are a two-parent family, make sure that you show a united front. The process of curtailing or eliminating video games from an adolescent child's life may be among the most challenging parent-child battles you will ever manage. Don't try it without first coming together with your spouse and planning your strategy. Even those who are divorced and sharing custody should attempt to agree on necessary steps in the best interest of the child. I suggest both Mom and Dad read this book as a first step toward a united front.

Second, invest in the relationship with your son or daughter before attempting to deal with his or her video game problem. Playing the authoritarian ruler can only hurt the situation, and possibly push away the children when you most need them to trust your judgment. Instead, take them to a movie, play catch, go shopping or camping or hiking or go-kart driving or miniature golfing. Whatever it takes, be sure to reconnect with your child before trying to disconnect the game system.

Third, thoroughly explain the problem. "Because I said so!" does not go over very well with adolescent kids. Take time to share the research with your children so that they understand the why before you implement the what. For parents who want help with this process, we have included an open letter to video game lovers as an appendix. In it we offer insight and advice from a recovering video game addict, explaining the risks and urging young people to avoid the path that led to his problems. In many instances the parent and child can craft a plan for avoiding addiction, giving the child ownership of the process and input into the plan of action.

Fourth, assume responsibility for the mistake. The child has done nothing wrong. We found it important to repeatedly assure Kyle that we were not upset with him, and that removing video games from our home was in no way punishment for his bad choices. Mom and Dad created the problem by failing to understand the addictive nature of games—and we apologized to him for allowing the problem to emerge.

Finally, invest in alternatives to make the transition easier. At first your child may find it difficult to imagine wanting to develop other hobbies or interests. But with a little parental help and financial backing, he will. (I've provided a list of alternatives at the end of this chapter.) If you decide to remove video games entirely, be prepared for a period of withdrawal requiring lots of patience and distractions. In our case we found ourselves investing in lots of books, games, radio dramas, and movie rentals. Over time, however, Kyle fell back into a normal, healthy pattern of interests. Before long, we found that we were spending about the same amount of money on alternatives that we had been spending on video games.

I offer the following suggested language for parents ready to have the important conversation with their adolescent child about video games:

- "We think you are mature enough to hear what we've learned about the addictive nature of video games and what steps we can take to prevent future problems in your life."
- "We owe you an apology for allowing video games to consume so much of your time and attention, and are committed to your happiness enough to build an action plan together."
- "Let's work together to help you find other activities that you will enjoy that do not lead to some of the problems other kids experience due to video game obsession."
- "During the first few months without video games at home it may be difficult for you because you might experience something called withdrawal from the games. So if

you are feeling depressed, tense, agitated, or resentful of this decision, let's discuss it. Such feelings are normal and will pass over time."

- "This may be a tense time in our relationship, so I promise that I will try to be patient whenever you want to talk about this decision—even when I feel frustrated. Please know that I am not angry at you, but angry at myself for letting the problem get so bad before addressing it."

- "How about if we schedule a night out once per week for your favorite activity [bowling, tennis, ice cream, a movie, etc.] to help ease the pain of this change."

Remember, the goal is to take responsibility for the problem yourself and communicate to your child that you are committed to helping him or her through the difficult transition. It is also important that you *be the parent,* since, in many cases, the child will do everything he or she can to get you to change your mind, to loosen the restrictions, or to feel even worse than you already do about the decision.

Be the parent, since, in many cases, the child will do everything he or she can to get you to change your mind, to loosen the restrictions, or to feel even worse than you already do about the decision.

A word about how to handle your child playing video games at the home of a friend. In reality, virtually every other kid will own a system, and your child will want to spend time at their houses in hopes of joining the fun. Because

removing the game system from our home eliminated 90 percent of the "easy access" problem, we have chosen to let our
children play while at a friend's house within reasonable time
constraints. I had to learn to become bold with other moms,
asking them to monitor and limit the time spent to one or two
hours per visit. Sometimes that can be an awkward conversation, especially when the other parent takes the kind of casual
approach to games I took before conducting this research. But
I find most share a similar apprehension about video games
and are interested to know more about the path we've chosen.

Teens and Young Adults

By the time a child reaches his midteen and early adult years,
digital game addiction may already be a serious problem af-
fecting other areas of life, such as school, college, work, and
relationships. My only advice to parents and loved ones is to
share the research and stories contained in this book and the
growing body of material coming out daily about video
game addiction. Teens and adults typically decide for themselves how to invest their time. To the degree you are able to
coach or guide that decision process, however, you may help
them avoid or break a cycle that carries negative long-term
consequences. Again, the open letter to video game lovers at
the end of this book may be a helpful first step. You might
also suggest that your child read the "True Confessions"
chapters. As with any other addictive pattern, the addict may
need the intervention of those who love him or her most—
perhaps a parent, sibling, wife, or close friend.

A special word to parents with kids heading off to college. It is vital that you address the problem of video game addiction on college campuses before your child heads off to school. This is especially true for boys. No matter how good their judgment and tendency to be good stewards of time, the culture of dorm life is a dangerous environment for those with even a remote draw to video games.

Another Life

The most common question parents ask me when they learn we no longer own a video game system is, "What do your kids do with their time?" On one hand, I find the question amusing. We forget that video games are a recent phenomenon in the annals of kid history, and that children managed to enjoy themselves before the advent of *Pong,* PlayStation, or Xbox. On the other hand, I find the question disturbing. It reveals just how far the digital drug has entrenched itself into our way of life. In my lifetime the microwave oven moved from novelty to necessity in the typical home. Video games have done the same, with millions of families unable to imagine life without them.

Michael Bugeja, director of the Greenlee School of Journalism and Communication, feels that it would be good for our children to return to a bygone era when parents couldn't imagine life with a video game system. In the past decade, Bugeja observes, "many children went from playing in parks in front of neighbors . . . to playing in mall arcades in front of parents . . . to playing in living-room consoles in front of each other . . . to playing online in their rooms in front of no one in a place that is actually not there."[2]

In her *New Atlantis* essay titled "Playgrounds of the Self," Harvard professor Christine Rosen critiques, among other things, the illusion that video games can actually be good for us: "To find the good in gaming . . . often requires strenuous leaps of logic and specious interpretations of the survey results."[3]

My friend Candice Watters, founding editor of Boundless webzine, captured the concerns and hopes many of us feel with regard to building a strong family identity. She said we should "encourage young families to proactively and intentionally develop a culture early on before video games are an issue. This takes a lot of time and means giving up weekend golf for hobbies the whole family can be a part of. But what a payoff! The analogy of a garden comes to mind. If you spend three, four, five years tilling and amending the soil, planting beautiful flowers and produce, and enjoying its bounty, why—when the garden is seven or eight years along—would you intentionally plant weeds?"

The world of video games can be a flat of weeds to the garden of your family culture. That is why I believe the time has come for moms and dads to become intentional about giving their kids another life. Not the few minutes of extended time rewarded through a high score on the latest digital game, or the artificial identity afforded by entering and conquering another virtual world, but a rich, satisfying life they can experience only in the real world God made for real people to enjoy. I believe parents have been given primary responsibility for nurturing children and guiding them toward sound, responsible life choices. Therefore, we must ask ourselves some commonsense questions:

- Do I feed my children a balanced, healthful diet or a constant stream of junk food?
- Do I teach my children to value the time they have been given?
- Do I make sure my kids brush their teeth and bathe, or do I let their teeth rot and bodies stink?
- Do I teach my children proper manners and respect for others, or do I laugh at their crude and rude behavior?
- Do I monitor their entertainment choices, or do I close my eyes to the kind of violence and filth commonly found on television screens, iPod playlists, and Internet search results?
- Do I take my kids to church to give them a spiritual foundation for life, or do I cross my fingers and hope they develop good values and beliefs?

Each question reflects a daily parental choice between leaving our kids to the vortex of irresponsibility and negative patterns, on the one hand, and leading them toward another kind of life, on the other. The kind every good parent wants his or her child to experience, but that requires more time, energy, and self-sacrifice to achieve.

When it comes to video games, the choice is equally important. We can either introduce our children to a wide array of wholesome activities that affirm and reinforce real life, or we can leave them to the addictive, life-draining snare of the digital drug.

For those who choose the former, creativity is a must. Sure, there was a time when video games were not an option and children used their imaginations when it came to finding hobbies and recreational activities. But many of our kids have already been conditioned with digital entertainment and need our help exploring other options.

So for those who may consider themselves creatively challenged I offer a short list of alternative activities to prime the idea pump. In addition, I provide links to other sources on my Web site, including special offers for those who subscribe to my free e-newsletter for moms. Visit me on the Web at www.VideoGameTrouble.org.

Alternative Activities

The fun part of helping your child break the video game habit is discovering the thousands of potential alternative activities he or she can enjoy. I recommend you identify five or six possible categories of interest for your child and invest the time and money necessary to explore options, trying them out until you find that perfect game, hobby, sport, book series, old television show DVD set, or whatever tickles your child's fancy.

The Internet can be a parent's best friend when it comes to finding alternatives. Here are a few companies to explore as you try to narrow down options for your child.

- Back to Basics Toys
- Highlights
- HearthSong
- Toys to Grow On
- Oriental Trading Company
- Young Explorers
- Usborne
- Klutz
- Games by James

Hobbies

I found a gold mine for parents seeking alternative entertainment when I visited our local hobby shop. I even spoke with an executive of a national chain called HobbyTown to get ideas. I love their corporate philosophy on product selection, as stated by Bob Wilke, HobbyTown USA senior vice president:

At HobbyTown USA our philosophy for selecting radio control vehicles, games, models and educational products is to provide renewable entertainment—fostering social interaction among friends and families, as well as offering stimulating challenges for individuals to expand their skills. While a case can be made for some positive aspects of video games, we find it does not mesh with our fundamental values of social interaction and stimulating play. Our stores do not offer video games, but rather offer real hobbies for real fun.[4]

"Real hobbies for real fun" is just the thing I wanted for my children, who had become consumed with "virtual games offering artificial satisfaction." It is important that parents turn the decision to decrease or eliminate video games into a positive experience, not just take away something to which the child has become attached. Explore the thousands of alternative recreational options with your children and give them an opportunity to choose fun, healthy, "real-life" hobbies. That is why I asked the folks at HobbyTown to provide the following list of alternatives for children at various ages and stages. They have also kindly offered a discount coupon to parents who visit my Web site to get you started exploring alternatives for your child, available at www.VideoGameTrouble.org.

PRESCHOOL
- Legos
- Play-Doh
- Wooden train sets
- Wooden puzzles
- Plastic play animals
- Fuzzy posters
- Playmobil toys
- Construction sets
- John Deere toys
- Classic wood toys—Lincoln Logs, Tinkertoys, etc.

- Marble Run construction sets
- Ant farms—the newest ones even glow in the dark!
- Dinosaur Dig activities
- Basic slot car sets

ELEMENTARY
- Science kits
- Marbles
- Yo-yos
- Action figures
- Erector sets
- Beginner rockets
- Simple kites
- Snap-together plastic model kits
- Slot car sets
- Electric radio control cars
- Foam glider planes
- Skyrail Marble Run sets
- Model railroad starter sets
- Puzzles
- HeroClix superheroes miniature games
- Mini–strategy games—Rush Hour, River Crossing, and more (great for car trips!)
- Beginner radio control boats
- Telescope with auto–star finder
- Art and craft sets
- Beadwork
- Face painting
- Dollhouse building

MIDDLE SCHOOL
- Photography
- Magic
- Cross-stitching
- Pottery
- Electric radio control trucks—both mini and large-scale
- Plastic and metal model kits—glue type
- Model railroad add-on sets, layout building supplies
- Ready-to-fly electric radio control airplanes
- Digital and multilane slot car sets
- Pirates miniature games
- Star Wars or sports-themed collectible card games
- Puzzles—3-D image, mosaic, or shaped
- Box or shaped kites
- Level 2 rockets
- Group games—Blockus, Apples to Apples, Fluxx, Blurt
- Simple robot construction kits
- Candle making or room decor kits
- Microscopes and science investigation kits

HIGH SCHOOL
- Risk: Lord of the Rings or miniature game
- Axis and Allies game or miniature game
- Nitro-powered radio control vehicles
- Radio control trainer plane or foam plane with combat features
- Collectible card games
- Military and auto model kits

- Digital command model railroad supplies
- Stunt kites
- Level 3 or multistage rockets
- Historical strategy games
- Challenging puzzles
- Construction sets with engines and electrical components
- Telescopes
- Metal detectors
- Leather and wood art sets
- Radio control boats

Reading

Give your children what author Gladys Hunt calls "honey for a child's heart" by helping them learn to love great books. (Her books are excellent resources that provide specific titles by age level.) Much of the time that my boys once spent in front of the screen is now spent turning pages, and I love it. Obviously, any local librarian or bookstore owner would be happy to help you identify great literature for every age. Here are a few book series that we found to be particularly good for our boys.

- The Chronicles of Narnia series by C. S. Lewis
- *The Hobbit* and *The Lord of the Rings* by J. R. R. Tolkien
- A Series of Unfortunate Events series by Lemony Snicket
- The Redwall series by Brian Jacques
- The Artemis Fowl series by Eoin Colfer
- The Inheritance series by Christopher Paolini
- Various historical fiction titles by G. A. Henty

Board Games

I often wonder how Parker Brothers, Hasbro, Milton Bradley, and the rest of the board game companies survive now that video games have overtaken the indoor recreational time of children. Why not discover some new games and rediscover old favorites with your children, starting with these:

- Stratego
- Chess and checkers
- Clue
- Monopoly
- Battle Ball
- Trivial Pursuit
- Risk
- Yahtzee
- Battleship
- Catch Phrase
- The Settlers of Catan (one of our new personal favorites)
- Memory
- Candy Land
- Blockus
- Make 'n' Break
- HeroScape

Card Games

Until my boys began searching for alternatives, I never knew just how many fun card games have been developed over the past decade. Again, they have proven a wonderful alternative to video games, fostering laughter and interaction among my boys and their friends rather than passive screen staring. I must caution you, however, that some card games have offensive or disturbing themes a parent should screen before purchase. Here are a few that we have found to be good, clean fun:

- The Star Munchkin series (Note: I did find it necessary to remove a few cards from the deck that I considered inappropriate.)
- Apples to Apples (original and junior versions)
- Pit
- Uno
- Skip-Bo
- Phase 10
- Quiddler
- Mille Bornes
- Split
- Model card games (Pirates is our boys' favorite—available at most hobby stores.)
- Traditional card games like Go Fish, Hearts, and Rummy

Sports
Several studies have shown a rising incidence of childhood obesity tied to declining physical activity, most notably among video game playing kids. So find a sport your children can enjoy and get them off their behinds!

- Baseball
- Basketball
- Soccer
- Martial arts
- Swimming
- Golf
- Tennis

Some fun alternatives for the less athletic child:
- Sport stacking (www.speedstacks.com)
- Table tennis
- Billiards
- Foosball
- Frisbee golf

Adventure Activities
Depending upon where you live, there are many ways your child can find adventure in the great outdoors.

- Hiking
- Camping
- Rock climbing
- Scouting
- Biking
- Fishing
- Snow fort building
- Snow skiing, snowboarding, or tubing
- Swimming
- Surfing
- Go-kart racing
- Dirt bike racing

DVDs

During the most difficult video game "withdrawal" period for our oldest son, he found watching DVDs of old television series helpful—a thirty-minute episode each evening, when he had been used to playing. It was just enough distraction to ease the suffering. It was also a great way to introduce him to some of our favorite old shows, like those in the following list. More recent shows are certainly an option, but we enjoyed introducing Kyle to a more innocent, wholesome era of television and film entertainment.

- *Gilligan's Island*
- *The Greatest American Hero*
- *Mork & Mindy*
- *The Andy Griffith Show*
- The Three Stooges
- The Marx Brothers
- *My Favorite Martian*
- *The Waltons*
- A thousand other choices available from Wal-Mart, Netflix, etc.

Audiobooks

Our children have always enjoyed listening to audio stories. Every local library makes audiobooks available, including some of the greatest literature ever penned. Once kids begin to listen, they won't want to stop. A great way to help children develop a taste for audio stories, in my opinion, is to listen to any of the following radio dramas:

- *Adventures in Odyssey* radio dramas (www.whitsend.org)
- *Jungle Jam* (ages four to ten)
- *Focus on the Family Radio Theatre* programs (www .radiotheatre.org), including the following stories:
  - *The Chronicles of Narnia*
  - *The Secret Garden*
  - *A Christmas Carol*
  - *Father Gilbert Mysteries*
  - *Les Misérables*
  - *Hiding Place*
  - *The Back of the North Wind*
  - *At Home in Mitford*

Educational Computer Games

There are a number of educational games for the computer that can be a good alternative to video games because of their lower risk of addiction, if carefully monitored and used for skill development. Our children, for example, enhanced their reading and math abilities with products obtained from the Learning Company. Look for games that teach reading, math, strategic thinking, typing, and other useful skills. The Tycoon series is a great one to try. War and strategy computer games are very popular and generally better than video games, but they do have some addictive qualities, such as requiring many hours to master.

Volunteer Services

In order to help children learn to engage real people in real life, partner with your children for some type of community service activity, pushing them beyond themselves into the joy (as opposed to "fun") of helping others. This might take a bit of effort on your part to discover the right opportunity for your family, but I've found you don't have to look far. A few ideas:

- Serve dessert at the local nursing home.
- Offer free babysitting for a single parent to give him or her a much-needed break.
- Contact local charities to learn what type of work children can do.
- Use the summers to get involved in your city's volunteer programs.

The above lists are just the tip of the iceberg. Once you begin the search, you will be amazed how many alternatives you will find. At first your children might snub every suggestion—in part because they don't know what they are missing. But I want to encourage you along the way. Consider me your cheerleader as you take the steps necessary to free your children from the addictive draw of the digital drug. You can awaken within them a love for real life!

Drop me a line to let me know how you are doing. And don't forget about my free e-newsletter offering encouragement, advice, and special offers for moms!

Contact Olivia Bruner at
www.VideoGameTrouble.org

AN OPEN LETTER TO THOSE WHO LOVE VIDEO GAMES

DEAR VIDEO GAME LOVER:
If you are reading or listening to this letter, it is probably because someone cares deeply about your happiness, health, and potential. Perhaps it is your mom, dad, a friend, or some other loved one. That person has discovered troubling information about video, Internet, and computer games and wants you to know how they can impact your life. We hope you will take these concerns seriously so that you can make wise decisions from this point forward.

You have probably heard that many video games contain violent, inappropriate, and dark themes. If you have played these games, you know what we mean. If you haven't played these games, good for you! Perhaps your parents have carefully monitored which games you have been allowed to play, protecting you from some pretty wretched stuff. Those who produce such games do not care about your well-being, happiness, or potential. They care only about selling as many games as possible, even if it means warping young minds.

Assuming you have managed to avoid such games, we want to explain an equally disturbing danger called video game addiction. A growing body of research shows that the brain reacts to video games similarly to the way it reacts to drugs, cigarettes, alcohol, gambling, and other forms of stimulation. Millions of people have become enslaved to these and other substances or behaviors for the same reasons kids and adults become addicted to video games. Let us briefly explain how this happens.

Playing video games triggers reactions in the human brain similar to those observed among animals seeking food or water. One scientist did an experiment with dogs, ringing a bell every time he served their food. After a while, ringing that bell caused them to salivate no matter the time—even if they were not hungry. The brain's habit continued because of something known as the law of reinforcement. Dogs associated the sound of the bell with food, making them crave it on cue.

Something similar occurs when we play video games regularly or for long periods. A chemical called dopamine begins flooding the brain after only about twenty minutes of video game play. This chemical is about the same as injecting an amphetamine into a person, creating a pleasurable "high" that makes the process addictive. Like the bell and the dogs, kids and adults alike easily become hooked on the feeling. That is why 20 to 25 percent of kids become addicted to video games.

We have interviewed a number of adults who became hooked on video games when they were younger and still struggle to overcome the addiction. They wish someone had read a letter like this to them before they became addicted. Maybe they could have avoided the many regrets—including thousands of hours of wasted time, years of diminished happiness, and countless squandered opportunities. Unfortunately, the research now available was not around when they were young.

You, on the other hand, have an opportunity to avoid making the same mistakes. We encourage you to start by asking those who know you best whether they think you spend too much time playing and talking about video games. Try not to be defensive. Listen with an open heart and mind, since they certainly want what is best for you.

Second, test yourself. Try putting all video, computer, and Internet games away for a month. If you find yourself repeatedly drawn back to them, wishing you could play, thinking and talking about them all the time, then you are probably already hooked, and it would be wise to get rid of them entirely. We encourage you to talk to your parents or someone you trust about helping you through the process. Like any other addiction, breaking this one will take courage and determination because it will involve a period of something called withdrawal—when you feel the emotional, physical, and social effects of stopping an addictive behavior. You may find yourself feeling depressed. That is because the "high" that came from playing games is no longer there. These feelings will pass, and you will eventually rediscover fun and joy apart from the games. Meanwhile, we encourage you to find several other activities you enjoy in order to distract yourself from the withdrawal symptoms.

Finally, replace the time you spend with video games with other, healthier recreational options. Develop a hobby, rent great movies, read good books, play board games, play a sport—you get the idea. There are a million ways you can spend your time. Believe it or not, people found plenty of fun things to do before video games were invented! The hard part, of course, will be that most if not all of your friends are heavily into these games, which could make you feel isolated or out of touch. If this is the case, you might want to read this same letter to your friends and invite them to explore new interests with you.

If you are unable to break the video game habit yourself, it might be necessary for your parents to make the decision for you. The former addicts I interviewed said that they wish their parents had done this for them, even though they would have been angry about it at the time. If your parents feel it necessary to make the tough call for you, please accept it with maturity—and recognize they only want what is best for you.

One thing we can say for certain: if you are able to break the video game habit now, you will be glad in years to come that you did. We guarantee that you will be happier and more successful by investing your time and talents in the true and lasting things around you rather than letting what we call the digital drug enslave you.

Kurt and Olivia Bruner

NOTES

FOREWORD

1. "Bedrooms Have Become Multi-Media Centers: Kids Say Parents Don't Set or Enforce Rules on Media Use." Kaiser Family Foundation News Release. Wednesday, March 9, 2005. http://www.kff.org/entmedia/entmedia030905nr.cfm.

2. Victoria Rideout, MA, Donald F. Roberts, PhD, and Ulla G. Foehr, MA, *Generation M: Media in the Lives of 8–18 Year-Olds.* Chapter 3. The Household Media Environment. Kaiser Family Foundation. Publication Number: 7250. March 9, 2005:6. www.kff.org/entmedia/upload/Generation-M-Media-in-the-Lives-of-8-18-Year-olds-Report-Section3.pdf.

3. Mark W. Merrill, "Life Without TV?" Family First. http://www.familyfirst.net/pressroom/lifewithouttv.asp.

4. "3 Ways TV Steals Kids' Time." WebMD News. February 6, 2006. http://www.webmd.com/content/Article/118/112962.htm.

5. Reported in Barbara J. Brock, "TV Free Families: Are They Lola Gra-

nolas, Normal Joes or High and Holy Snots?"; can be viewed on the Web at www.tvturnoff.org/brock2.htm.

INTRODUCTION

1. www.PS3Land.com/news/article40.php.

2. http://www.mediafamily.org/research/report_vgrc_2002-2.shtml.

3. http://www.mediafamily.org/facts/facts_gameaddiction.shtml.

CHAPTER 2

1. Chris Richard, "Addicted Gamers, Losing Their Way," *Washington Post,* January 5, 2004.

2. Joshua Quittner, "Are Video Games Really So Bad?" *Time Asia,* May 10, 1999, www.time.com/time/asia/asia/magazine/1999/990510/video1.html.

3. Ibid.

4. Ibid.

5. "Video Games: Cause for Concern?" *BBC News Online,* November 26, 2000, http://news.bbc.co.uk/1/hi/uk/1036088.stm#top.

6. Alison Motluk, "Gaming Fanatics Show Hallmarks of Drug Addiction," *New Scientist,* November 2005, http://www.newscientist.com/article.ns?id=dn8327&feedId=online-news_rss20.

7. Ibid.

8. Ricardo A. Tejeiro Salguero and Rosa M. Bersabe Moran, "Measuring Problem Video Game Playing in Adolescents," *Addiction* 97, no. 12 (December 2002): 1601.

9. Linda A. Johnson, "Video Games Better Than Tranquilizers at Keeping Children Calm before Surgery, Study Finds," Associated Press, December 9, 2004, http://www.msnbc.msn.com/id/6687019/.

10. David Sheff, *Game Over: How Nintendo Zapped an American Industry, Captured Your Dollars, and Enslaved Your Children* (New York: Random House, 1993), 205.

11. Jay Ingram, "Positron Emission Tomography," EXN.ca, Discovery Channel Online, June 12, 1998.

12. *Nature,* 393 (May 1998): 266.

13. Ibid.

14. MediaWise Video Game Report Card, 2004, National Institute on Media and the Family, www.mediafamily.org.

CHAPTER 4

1. Geoff Howland, "Game Design: The Addiction Element," 1999, www.gamedev.net/reference/articles/article263.asp. Mahboubeh Asgari, "A Three-Factor Model of Motivation and Game Design" (Faculty of Education, Simon Fraser University, April 16, 2005), www.gamesconference .org/digra2005/viewabstract.php?id=269.

2. Michael Snider, "Wired to Another World," *Maclean's* 116, no. 9 (March 2003).

3. *The Jane Pauley Show,* ABC, May 19, 2005, www.thejanepauleyshow .com/aboutshow/20050519.html.

4. Gerald G. May, MD, *Addiction and Grace* (New York: Harper SanFrancisco, 1988).

5. Ibid., p. 75.

6. Ibid., p. 78.

7. Ibid., p. 86.

8. Ibid., pp. 13–14.

9. Rideout et al., *Generation M.*

10. Mark Rutland, *Behind the Glittering Mask* (Ann Arbor: Servant Publications, 1996), 111.

11. Ibid., p. 110.

12. Ibid.

CHAPTER 6

1. Tom Chiarella, "The Lost Boys," *Esquire* 141, no. 2 (February 2004): 84.

2. Ibid.

3. Ibid.

4. Ibid.

5. Ibid.

6. John G. Messerly, "The Impact of Video Games on College (Particularly Computer Science) Students," *Communications of the ACM* 47, no. 3 (March 2004): 29.

7. Ibid.

8. Chiarella, "The Lost Boys."

CHAPTER 8

1. "Computer Games Kill 12-Year-Old," WorldNetDaily.com, June 23, 2005.

2. "S. Korean Man Dies after 50 Hours of Computer Games," Reuters, August 9, 2005.

3. "Addicted: Suicide over EverQuest?" *Prime Time*, CBS News, October 18, 2002, www.cbsnews.com/stories/2002/10/17/48hours/main 525965.shtml.

4. Snider, "Wired to Another World."

5. Nicholas Yee, "Ariadne—Understanding MMORPG Addiction," October 2002, www.nickyee.com.

CHAPTER 9

1. "Can a Video Game Lead to Murder?" *60 Minutes,* CBS News, June 19, 2005, www.cbsnews.com/stories/2005/06/17/60minutes/printable 702599.shtml.

2. Ibid.

3. Oliver Stallwood, "New Warning over Violent Video Games," *Evening Standard* (London), Associated New Media, June 23, 2005, www.thisislondon.co.uk/londoncuts/articles/19490106?source=Metro.

4. "Less Videogame Violence Is Urged," *Wall Street Journal,* August 18, 2005.

5. Jeff Hooten, "Point. Click. Kill," *Focus on the Family Citizen Magazine,* February 2006, 24.

6. 2005 MediaWise Video and Computer Game Report Card, www.mediafamily.org.

7. Kevin Haninger, M. Seamus Ryan, and Kimberly M. Thompson, MS, ScD, "Violence in Teen-Rated Video Games," *Medscape General Medicine* 6, no. 1 (2004).

CHAPTER 10

1. Rideout, Roberts, and Foehr, *Generation M.*

2. Christine Rosen, "Playgrounds of the Self," *New Atlantis,* Summer 2005.

3. Rosen, p. 25.

4. Karey Koehn, ed., *HobbyTown USA's Hobby Outlook Magazine.* Used by permission.

ABOUT THE AUTHORS

Kurt and Olivia Bruner are in the middle of what they call "the mini-van years" with their own four children. As featured authors and speakers for The Heritage Builders Association, the Bruners inspire parents to celebrate the hectic joys of parenting and become intentional about giving a strong heritage to the next generation.

A former sixth-grade teacher, Olivia directs the Video Game Trouble project (www.videogametrouble.org). Olivia is a popular speaker for parents and educators and has been a frequent guest on the Focus on the Family broadcast.

Kurt is a graduate of Talbot Seminary who served as group vice president over media for Focus on the Family, where he led the teams creating films, magazines, books, and radio dramas such as *Adventures in Odyssey* and *The Chronicles of Narnia*. Kurt is a speaker and best-selling author of books with combined sales of over 500,000 copies, including *Your Heritage* and The Family Night Tool Chest series.

ALSO BY OLIVIA AND KURT BRUNER

The Family Compass

ALSO BY KURT BRUNER

Finding God in the Land of Narnia

The Marriage Masterpiece
(coauthored with Al Janssen)

Inklings of God: What Every Heart Suspects

Parents' Guide to the Spiritual Growth of Children
(coauthored with John Trent and Rick Osborne)

The Divine Drama: Discovering Your Part in God's Story

Finding God in the Lord of the Rings

*Your Heritage: How to Be Intentional about
the Legacy You Leave*
(coauthored with J. Otis Ledbetter)

Responsible Living in the Age of Excuses

The Family Night Tool Chest series